Passions of a Poet

Andrea Lippi

To Marlin Bennetch
Best Wishes
Catherine Lippi
Enjoy!

Lippi Publishing, LLC
Box 188, Goshen, New Jersey 08218
www.AndreaLippiPoet.com

Passions of a Poet

A glimpse at the life and poetry of a devoted American

Andrea Lippi

Written and composed by
Maria and Michael Kane

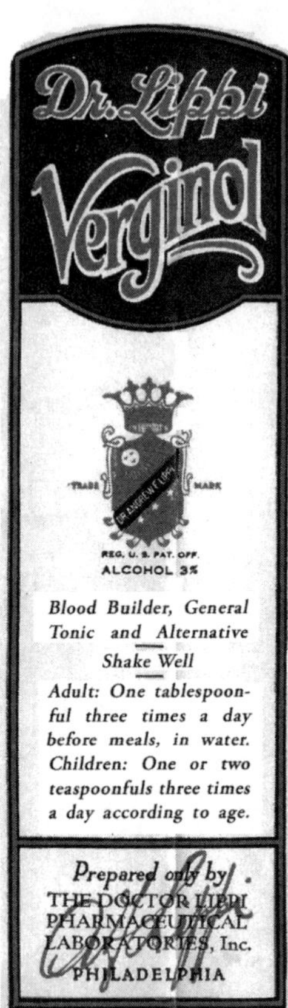

Andrea Lippi's father was a pharmacist in Philadelphia who, like many pharmacists at that time, prepared his own "cure-all" tonic. This is the bottle label from Dr. Lippi's own blend.

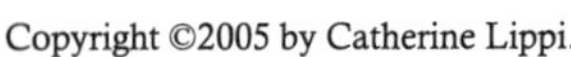

Copyright ©2005 by Catherine Lippi.

ISBN 0-9771729-0-2

First Printing, 2006

Published by Lippi Publishing, LLC

Printed by Sheridan Books, Inc., Ann Arbor, MI U.S.A.

Dedicated to my beloved husband, Andrea.
May his soul now accompany the Almighty
as he flies on the wings of the wind.

When Mrs. Lippi first approached us with the idea of creating this book, we were delighted, for we knew Mr. Lippi personally and had grown quite fond of him. Even though we knew him for a relatively short period of time, we admired him for his love of life and the positive energy he radiated. Little did we know how deep his strength and devotion was throughout his entire life.

In a world striving for materialistic wealth, Mr. Lippi never had "riches" in mind and strived only to make a difference. He preferred to live of simple means but with a quality of life rich in passion, love and excitement. His 'cup was always half full', and he exuded that outlook in everything he did. He was a spiritual man who faithfully appreciated all that came his way - and that is refreshing.

We are grateful to Catherine for sharing such treasured details and stories of her husband's life and for giving us the opportunity to learn more about this man, who motivated us and changed our lives. We only hope that we did him justice and composed this book, as he would have, in a fun and playful style. We incorporated many pictures for visual understanding, and out of the thousands of poems we had to choose from, we hope you will enjoy the ones in this book.

May you draw enjoyment and inspiration as you read about Andrea: a Poet with an extraordinary personality.

Passions of a Poet

Andrea Lippi

Contents

A. Lippi

Introduction

Andrea Lippi was one of the most colorful people of our time and place in history. A spirited man, if you will, Andrea chose to create his own life rather than have it created for him. He lived his dream – far from riches and monetary goals – but towards personal fulfillment and humanitarian efforts.

Born in South Philadelphia in 1918 of Italian descent, Andrea became a poet the night his father died in 1951. Words started to flow from his soul onto paper, and at that moment, he felt his calling. When most of us would contemplate finances, Andrea turned his back on a successful business career, and at the age of 33, changed the way he would spend his time.

Fundamentally, he was a poet – and a good one – always on a quest for inspiration, writing of things that interested him and that moved his psyche. Andrea attended evening school with great persistence and obtained his Doctorate degrees in Romantic Literature and Theology. He threw himself into the public eye, focusing on his talents as a poet, a journalist and a storyteller. In his daily life, he incorporated the things he was most passionate about, wanting only the opportunity to share his experiences, while entertaining others and broadening their minds. He would sit for hours with total strangers, telling stories about his adventures and charming his listeners with his eccentric personality. He had boundless energy, always proclaiming his love of country, the sea, his world travels, his compassion for the armed forces and children, to name only a few. With a stature of no more than 5½ feet and with the kindest of eyes, his charming and inspirational qualities made him quite memorable.

In the prime of his life, Andrea wrote poetry, owned and published two newspapers and had a weekly TV program covering art, travel, poetry and people. This provided him the plane ticket to his next destination. He traveled around the world numerous times, stopping off at the most fascinating places, sharing his poetry and promoting his country, collecting pictures and film, all to make interesting reading and storytelling.

He did *what* he wanted, *when* he wanted and did things, he claimed, when the spirit moved him, always with a mind-set of excitement and joy. He had such strong faith, that he lived without worry, knowing that God would provide. He chose to live a simple and honest life, unfussy and without greed, and he awoke blissfully happy and grateful for every day.

Andrea was a hopeless romantic and was in love with his wife for over 30 years. He found solace and inspiration in Catherine, and she, in turn, found enjoyment in his spontaneous nature. For instance, if "Big-Band" music started playing on the car radio, he was known to pull over, turn up the volume and dance with his wife on the side of the road.

Andrea was constantly writing, jotting down a poem on anything that was around; a paper plate, a napkin, or the back of a receipt. He was the worst speller - and knew it - but was never discouraged from writing and always kept a dictionary close by. He wrote poetry every night religiously at around 3:00 in the morning, whether it was at the kitchen table or by the window, always by candlelight, feeling a connection with the Heavens. With discipline and love for what he was doing, he wrote his thoughts for the evening, and poems were born, keeping them easy enough for all to enjoy.

He wrote over 2000 poems in his lifetime, some being published around the world and in several languages. He took thousands of still pictures, gathered hundreds of hours of taped recordings and reel upon reel of motion picture film. He managed to be in the most interesting places at just the right time. Whether on a Mediterranean cruise with the New York Mets, a front-row seat at the blast-off of Apollo 11, or sharing poetry with Muhammad Ali, his life's experiences resulted in interesting material and thought-provoking poetry.

In his later years, he kept the 'look of a gentleman' with an artist's flair, as he loved to wear his Amethyst beads. A true Renaissance Man of our time, Andrea was rich in *charisma* and *genuine kindness*.

This book holds just a glimpse of the fascinating life Andrea led, what inspired him, the places he visited, and the legend he left behind.

When the cares of the day, 'are not over'
But the sun sinks in the west

And you sit down on your easy chair
To counsel with God – then rest!!

May the poems in this book give you pleasure
Paint pictures, which bring you delight

May you sleep and the angels watch over you
May the 'morrow be cheerful and bright

∾ Andrea ∾

This introductory poem was written by Andrea Lippi
in anticipation of his next book of poetry.

A. Lippi

$\mathcal{E}$ven though Andrea dealt with a variety of issues throughout his life, his fulltime love was Robert Louis Stevenson. When Andrea Lippi was a young boy, he read Stevenson's *Treasure Island* and dreamed of going there as he watched the ships go by from the family's beachside vacation home in Longport, NJ. Andrea was so inspired and personally affected by Stevenson's tales, it is safe to say, his entire life became molded by it.

Even in his later years, he wrote poems of Stevenson's Treasure Island, and wherever there was a crowd of children, he would sit with them and tell of its story and recite his rhymes:

TO TREASURE ISLAND

MAJESTIC TREASURE ISLAND
YOU'RE PROUD AS YOU CAN BE,
EMPRESS OF AN OCEAN,
JEWEL OF A TROPIC SEA.

WHO WILL KNOW YOUR SECRET?
WHO WILL KNOW YOUR LOVE?
THERE WILL COME A TRAVELER,
SENT BY GOD ABOVE.

Again to Treasure Island

Again to Treasure Island
Through the pages of endless time.
Again to Treasure Island,
To the boyhood dreams of mine.

To a far off tropic island,
Where the gold is buried deep;
To a far off tropic island,
Where the hills are high and steep.

There I find the buccaneers,
From story books of old –
Sit there by a glowing fire,
Where new tales will unfold.

Then I return to the homeland,
To tell the stories true –
Sit by a glowing fire,
And tell of adventure new.

Andrea Lippi was quite intrigued by Robert Louis Stevenson and studied him in depth; even writing his doctorate on his life. He researched Stevenson so extensively that, "Sometimes his life seems so familiar that I feel as if I were living it myself", he was quoted as saying.

Whenever anyone would ask Andrea about Stevenson, he would speak of him as if he were a friend. He studied his life, works, family and travels. He discovered that the Stevenson's family built lighthouses and even wrote a poem in dedication to the Stevenson heritage:

Builders of Light Houses

All were we
That is all, all except me

J built dreams and stories rare
Tales of pirates with doubloons to spare

Dr. Jekyll and Mr. Hyde
Taken in stride

Now once more through time, with grace
J find myself with the human race

Building lighthouses as J wish
Even lighthouses on a dish

A dish that will sail through time and space
May J present this to your grace

Andrea mentions "a dish" as he designed several plates made in traditional Delft Blue earthenware, displaying his poems and designs, which he had made in Holland.

Andrea felt there were many similarities with their lives: Both were ex-law students turned poets, with boyish qualities and a thirst for exploration. Both were men who loved the sea and were incurably in love with the romantic side of things. Andrea was a believer in karma and "psychic instruction" and suspected the spirit of Stevenson inspired his writings. He was convinced that his "life and creative powers" were linked to him in some way.

In 1956, Andrea could wait no longer. Serving as an ambassador of Good Will for the Port of Philadelphia and carrying introductory letters from city officials, he set out on a six-month pilgrimage to trace Stevenson's footsteps, in particular, his trip to the South Seas.

In 1888, Robert Louis Stevenson had already achieved a literary reputation, which included *Dr. Jekyll* and *Mr. Hyde*, and was financially comfortable. Because of his ill health, Stevenson decided to sail the South Seas to look for a warmer climate. Stevenson and his wife, Fanny, made arrangements to set sail from San Francisco on the sailing yacht, Casco, for an extended sailing trip. Andrea had a deep passion for the Casco and wrote many poems telling of its journey. He even wrote a poem telling of Manasquan, New Jersey, where Stevenson lived for a short period of time for the sake of fresh air and boating. This was where the Stevensons started their search for a sailing vessel for his South Sea voyage, and they eventually found one in San Francisco.

Was in Manasquan

Was in Manasquan by the bay and sea
Where Stevenson lived most happily

Walking the beaches enjoying the pines
Composing poems reciting rhymes

Then a wire was sent by his lady fair
Inviting him to the south sea air

The Schooner Casco was ready to sail
It was the start of an enchanting tale

Tusitala of the South Seas

Schooner Casco

T'was the Schooner Casco
That sailed the southern seas
Crossing the equator
To the far New Hebrides

Samoa and Tahiti
Islands in the blue
Captain Otis was the skipper
Of the very skillful crew

Robert Louis Stevenson
Was master of the realm
Taking his chosen turn
At the Schooner's helm

Now the Schooner Casco
Sailed among the stars
On the seas of yesteryear
In the fondest dreams of ours

This poem of the Casco is written with such endearing words, you can feel Andrea's passion for the voyage:

Heaven's Ship

A ship sailed up the river
That all the good could see,
And Oh what a ship – was this wonderful ship,
The finest that ever could be.

Its masts were white hard ivory,
Sails all spun of gold,
And of this ship, this wonderful ship,
Were wondrous stories told.

She sailed from a port in heaven,
To a port where good men live,
And when you see this blessed ship,
A Blessing it will give.

So always remember the story,
And keep this thought in mind –
When you sail off to heaven's shore,
This ship you are sure to find.

It was very important for Andrea to write "in the Stevenson style", as he liked to call it. He tried to capture this by going on a literary journey to the South Pacific as Stevenson had. Andrea, who financed the trip himself, visited places which included the sites where Stevenson was born, lived, traveled and died. Andrea wanted to absorb the ingredients of Stevenson's style of writing. When asked what made him take this journey, he simply stated, "Something told me to do it. It was as if Stevenson spoke to me….and besides, a man must always have a mission in life." He truly felt that this was a "calling".

❧ *Tahiti* ❧

Andrea's adventure started in Philadelphia from where he flew to Panama. There he boarded the French ship, Resurgent, sailing for Tahiti. Tahiti was also the first place Stevenson visited in the South Seas. For the next three and a half weeks, using all the research he had in his memory, he looked for the places Stevenson went to on the island of Tahiti.

Andrea was also captivated by the Polynesian beauty and was so enthused, he wrote many poems about Tahiti. Here are a few:

HONEYMOON IN TAHITI

HONEYMOON IN TAHITI
'NEATH THE SWAYING PALMS
MUSIC OF THE ISLANDS
WORDS FROM THE BOOK OF PSALMS

HOURS OF BLISS ON A STARRY NIGHT
BY A TRANQUIL SEA
HEAVEN HERE ON EARTH
HOURS OF ECSTASY

Tahiti

The Angels dwell upon the sea
On an isle near Tahiti

The diadem in splendor shows
Just why or when, all heaven knows

So say a prayer beside the sea
That you might visit Tahiti.

A. Lippi

Quinns of Tahiti

Quinns is the place where palm trees sway
You can sit on the porch
The live-long day

Coconut cake, coconut pie
Coconut ice cream
Piled to the sky

Music fills the very air
Easy life
Without a care

Shipmates meet from the world around
You have not lived
Till Quinns you have found

While in Tahiti, Andrea met and befriended Tony A. Bambridge, a Tahitian businessman, who owned hotels and theatres on the island. Fired by Andrea's enthusiasm over the "South Pacific teller of tales", Bambridge dedicated a park in Stevenson's honor on land he owned and on which Stevenson's "little grass shack" stood. Bambridge and Lippi joined in the dedication of the Robert Louis Stevenson Park Foundation. Andrea was very proud of this tribute.

Andrea wrote this next poem on his stay in Tahiti, and Tony Bambridge published the poem for him on a postcard with original Tahitian artwork. Andrea sent the poems back to the States and Europe:

Lovely Moorea

Moorea is more than an Island
It is part of the Sunset's glow
Jewel of Tropic flavor
That all Tahitians know

Engulfed in Heavenly beauty
Blessed by Heavenly charms
Lovely, Lovely Moorea
Did Venus spring from your arms?

Andrea was so inspired by the beauty of Tahiti and its spectacular sunsets, that during the hours before he left the island, he jotted down these words and left them with a friend:

It isn't often that I cry
Or let the tears fall from my eye
But Tahiti you must know
That for you the tears will flow

Wondrous Tropic Island
Where fondest dreams come true
My happy heart is heavy
As I sail away from you

❧ *Samoa* ❧

Next, Andrea visited Samoa where the Stevensons fell in love with the island and its people. Robert and Fanny purchased land and built a house and made quite the happy home. This is where Stevenson spent the last years of his life. Andrea visited the home, called *Valimar*, that has since been converted to a museum. He wrote a poem of Stevenson's journey to Samoa and the place he made his home:

Stevenson's Schooner Casco

Stevenson's Schooner Casco sailed away,
Sailed from Frisco Bay,
To take the Author Stevenson
To Samoa far away.

Her skipper, Captain Otis
Did guide the stately ship.
Robert and his family
Enjoyed the wondrous trip.

She put into Tahiti,
Then sailed the sea so blue.
Apia, Samoa received a son.
Quite true.

Valimar was his mansion,
Mount Via his estate.
He sails the Heavens among the stars
They spoke of him of late.

The Queen came to Samoa,
To visit the sunny isle.
Angels sang and natives danced
And Stevenson did smile.

Andrea also made the hike to the Stevenson grave. He climbed high up to the top of the jungle-clad Mt. Vaea, up a rough path that finally lead to a clearing where you can see the island of Upselu and its breaking surf in all directions. It was a breathtaking sight. There, in the center of that clearing, were the simple tombs of Stevenson and Fanny. On their graves he placed a wreath of flowers and paid his respects. One can only imagine the emotion Andrea felt to be at the resting place of his inspirational mentor.

Stevenson's life abruptly ended on December 3, 1894 of a brain hemorrhage at the age of 44. His epitaph reads:

> *Under the wide and starry sky*
> *Dig the grave and let me lie,*
> *Glad did I live and gladly die*
> *And I laid me down with a will.*
> *This be the verse you grave for me.*
> *Here he lies where he longed to be*
> *Home is the sailor, home from the sea.*
> *And the hunter home from the hill.*

Andrea felt so overwhelmed at Stevenson's tomb that he "was inspired to write a poem to him" then and there:

High on a Hill

High on a hill
Up near heaven
Above a tropic sea

Lies the dust of a man
Who loved the Lord
An angel now he be

Chief and friend
Of the people
Donor to mankind

When we go to Heaven
Stevenson
We will find

While in Samoa, Andrea visited and interviewed old native chieftains who had known Stevenson personally. He was happy to see that "the people's reverence of him almost amounts to adoration". "The memory of Robert Louis Stevenson was still very much alive in the islands, and they still referred to him as "Tusitala" – the teller of tales."

Fiji

From Samoa Andrea went to the Fiji Islands where he presented a "key" from the Old Swedes church called Gloria Dei in Philadelphia to the Right Rev. Stanley Leonard Kempthorn, Anglican Bishop of Polynesia. The "key" was given to Lippi by the Rev. Dr. John Craig Roak, rector of Gloria Dei, and Gen. J. Alex Crothers, head of the Delaware River Port Authority as a token of good will on behalf of Delaware Valley, USA.

After leaving Fiji, Andrea's journey took him to New Zealand, Australia, Arabia, Egypt, Italy, Switzerland, France, Germany, Belgium, Holland…..

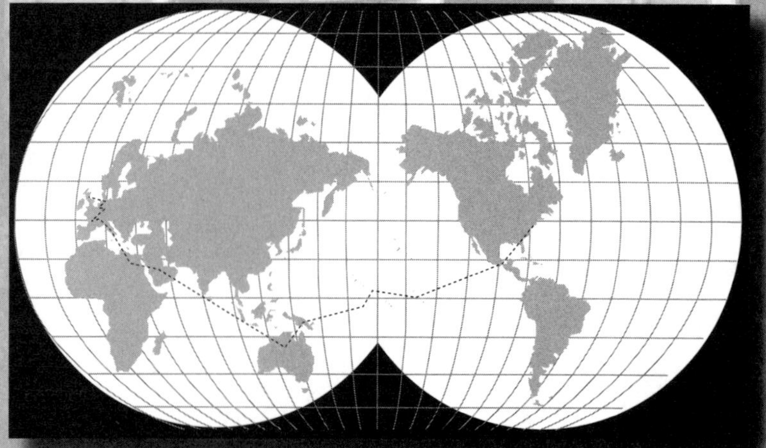

....And finally, to Edinburgh, Scotland, the birthplace and boyhood home of Stevenson. After almost seven months, this was the end of Andrea's odyssey and the most anticipated.

"By plane and ship, I at last stood in the room in which he was born."

Andrea Lippi, a latter-day pilgrim, following in the steps of a literary giant. Inspired by one man, Andrea had taken up a career in writing, wrote and published books of poems and traveled around the world, all to capture the personality of one Robert Louis Stevenson.

ndrea had many official titles reflecting a lifetime of accomplishments, but there was an unofficial title he held that really reflected best who he was as a person – Papa Noel. The one accomplishment he was most proud of involved a red suit, a zoo of stuffed animals and, most importantly, a group of enthusiastic children of all ages, as seen in the picture above taken in Valkenburg, Holland.

His role as Santa was one of the most pleasurable experiences for him personally. He spent many hours preparing and organizing such a large philanthropic deed. His role as "the patron saint of the toyless" gives a look into his true heart and selfless nature. He so much enjoyed the role and the joy it brought to the children that he continued to play Santa for more than 40 years both in the States and abroad.

A. Lippi

'Santa' Lippi, laden with bags, bundles and boxes of toys, with his head full of rhymes and poems, dazzled the children who met him. He went out of his way to visit and bring toys to children who were less fortunate or handicapped. Whether it was the children from St. John's Orphanage in Philadelphia, the Betty Bacharach Home in Longport, the Seashore House in Atlantic City, Burdette Tomlin Memorial Hospital in CMCH, NJ and even as high up as in the mountains of the historic town of Tolox in Spain, Andrea always had his toy bag packed and ready to go. "I love doing this", he said, "It makes life worthwhile to see the faces of those youngsters and how happy it makes them to be recognized."

When Andrea first started this venture, he contacted John Wanamaker from Philadelphia who was a lifelong friend. He made arrangements with Mr. Wanamaker to donate toys for the children for his Santa mission. Later, he began to gather toys on his own throughout the year so that he would always be ready for the holidays. He and his wife would spend many hours buying toys and collecting them from donators to get them ready for his Christmas mission. Hundreds of stuffed animals, dolls, toy boats and trains would be packed in crates and suitcases ready to make their trip. Andrea was especially fond of stuffed animals and boats because they always seemed to bring the biggest smiles to the children and comfort them more than anything else. From his year-round efforts in gathering toys, he emerged with the idea of creating the World Toy Bank, a non-profit corporation that would accumulate used toys, to be given to the children of the less fortunate all over the globe. Andrea and the Cathedral Parish School in St. Augustine, Florida were the first "depositors" to the bank. "If I can inspire a million people to save five toys during the year, that would be five million toys, and that could go to a lot of children", he said. Andrea always had faith in humankind. He once said, "We'll count on it starting in one place – in the hearts of man. That will make all the difference."

Andrea even wrote a poem about his quest for toys. He called it "The Eternal Toy", and it goes like this:

The Eternal Toy

Please don't throw your toys away
For with other children they would play.

Toys have feelings just as you
So treat them as a friend so true.

Find them a home when you must go
And other children their love will know.

Toys are angels in disguise
Born to lighten children's eyes,

Sure to make a happy place
For everyone who sees their face.

While Andrea's Santa role started as a local effort in Philadelphia and the Jersey Shore, it was not long before Santa was traveling to Appalachia and overseas. Because of his traditional nature, he would start his annual journey to Europe from the deck of the Schooner America in Cape May. He chose this ship because it so closely resembled the Schooner Casco, which brought Robert Louis Stevenson to the South Sea Islands. Dressed as Santa and carrying a full satchel, he would present toys to the children of the fisherman who he felt were often forgotten during the holidays when business was slow. Then, still wearing his bright red suit and fluffy white beard, he would head off to the airport with his sack of toys. He would board the airplane, enchanting everyone on board. "The passengers on the plane all love it", he said. "When they get off the plane, they can say they flew with Santa on one of his trips."

Captain Santa aboard the Schooner America in Cape May Harbor.

Santa and The Seaman

Santa Claus came on the bridge
And had a chat with me,
"Mate," he said, "please let me know
What I can do for thee."

My kids are home, quite all alone,
My lady has gone to rest,
Their granny sits in my house
I wish you would be their guest.

With just a chuckle, he was off!
His reindeer touched our spars,
I watched his sleigh, as it did streak
And dance among the stars.

Back home in a little village
In a cottage by the sea,
There was dear old granny
Crying desperately.

A knock then came upon the door
And much to her surprise,
There was Santa Claus himself
Looking in her eyes.

"Cry not, good soul, I come to you
To change your Christmas plight."
And there upon the very spot
Toys piled up, out of sight.

When morning came, the kids were wild
And as pleased as they could be.
Their daddy spoke to Santa Claus
While sailing o'er the sea.

Andrea had a special place in his heart for Spain. "When I'm there, I walk around the streets and sing." "I felt that I would like to repay Spain for all the happiness that it has given me." However, Andrea felt that children all over the world had an equal need for some happiness in their lives, and it was his mission in life to bring it to them, especially those who were "the forgotten ones". "I hope in the future, as my resources increase, to step up my activities and visit more and more children and bring them the love I have been able to bring to the children of Spain." He was quoted as saying, "I am a poet and poems are for children…". The simplicity of his poems reflect how much he wanted children, as well as adults, to enjoy his work and inspirational message.

He had a personal love for the youngsters at the Aspromanis School in Malaga for underprivileged children, and nothing pleased him more than bringing a smile to their faces. It was his annual visits to the special needs school that brought him the title Papa Noel. "It's as much fun for me as it is for the children I give the gifts to, except you have to *multiply* their pleasure to come anywhere near what I feel."

Three Wise Men

Wise men knew when they saw the star
They would travel very very far

Further than the manger of the king
For even today a message they bring

Peace on Earth, Good will toward men
Open your hearts again and again

Spread the message of Christmas and good cheer
Thank God for Christmas every year

To the children of Spain, he was better known as "the patron saint of the toyless". One of his favorite and most successful areas he visited was a town high up in the mountains of Malaga, Spain, where it was so remote, you had to drive the car up a hill of stairs to reach the town. As remote as it was, children were plentiful, and they would all gather to await the American Santa. "The children of Tolox just went wild. They had to have policemen around just to keep things orderly", wrote one of the local papers.

Christmas

Angels sang, the world stood still
A brilliant star shone over the hill
Jesus born in Bethlehem
Peace on Earth, Good Will to Men

Stars remember that sacred night
To the world was born a guiding light
Jesus, Savior. Jesus, King.
On this Christmas night, of thee we sing

Christmas In Torremolinos

Christmas In Torremolinos
Beside the Spanish Sea
Let me just say
That's the place to be

Santa and his reindeer
They like it best
On the beaches they can dream
And also quietly rest

All the children
Happy as can be
So many gifts
Oh, what a sight to see

Make your plans
To trim the Christmas tree
Torremolinos...
That's the place for me

Presented to Mayor Pedro Fernandez Montes
and the People of Torremolinos.

It Was The Eve Before Christmas

It was the eve before Christmas
The castle was bare
Scrooge was debunked
And Santa was there

The toys and the children
Yet hadn't met
The reindeers and Rudolph
Were all in a sweat

Then all of a sudden
There was a great change
The cowboys all started
To sing Home On The Range

Tonto and Silver
All saved the day
The children delighted
When the toys came their way.

Andrea always went out of his way to make sure that he could make a difference in the lives of children at Christmas. Whether it was the special needs children at the Aspromanis School, the ones in Aviles, Spain (the sister-city of St. Augustine, Florida), those in Tolox City in Andalucia, Spain, the children in Appalachia, or even the children of the fishermen in Cape May Harbor, Papa Noel was there for them to spread some joy at Christmas.

Christmas Prayer

O Lord, give me a Christmas Prayer
That I might say, and then be there

In Bethlehem, that sacred night
To search the sky, and see the light

Then find the manger of the King
Of Heaven oh, – what joys would ring

Mary, Joseph and the Child
And the animals that rest awhile

The Wise Men did their gifts unfold
This story to the world behold

Of Christmas and a joyous day
What better gift than an hour to pray.

Papa Noel

Andrea Lippi distributing toys at the Betty Bacharach Home where they were greeted by Longport, NJ Mayor, Leon Leopardi

Capt. Santa

Santa is a pilot
Who flies
The Christmas skies

Spreading joy
Around the world
An angel in disguise

Flying folks
And families
Gifts and toys galore

Santa is a pilot
May he fly
Forevermore

Landing in Malaga, Spain

At the controls of a TWA jet just before take-off
with Captain Phillip Rimmier

Christmas in Old Cape May

Christmas Night
In Old Cape May
Santa perched
Up on his sleigh

Loaded down with
Wondrous toys
For all the girls
And all the boys

Reindeers resting
In a mall
Place they like
The most of all

Gaslights glow
The night away
Joyous carols
Come our way

Church bells ring
The organ plays
Reminds you of
The bygone days

Christmas Night
In Old Cape May
For peace on earth
We solemnly pray

A. Lippi

Remember Santa

Always remember
There is a Santa Claus
And he lives
At the north pole

Always remember
There is a Santa
Of him
Are stories told

Santa and the spirit
Of Christmas
Do surely, encompass
The earth

Good jolly
Santa Claus
God does know
His worth

Distributing toys to over 500 children that gathered
in Tolox, Spain, 1979

The children would beam with delight at his Santa Claus suit, his toys and his rhymes. Andrea was happiest surrounded by those children. Three, four, five hundred children would gather around him, with arms outstretched, eagerly wanting to be near him and receive his gift. This is where Papa Noel felt the most gratification.

ndrea Lippi loved the water and was never very far away from it. In his years as a young man, when he wasn't working, he would cruise in his 30-foot Chris Craft up and down the Jersey coast, occasionally fishing, but mostly, getting energized from the sea and salt air.

Andrea had such a feeling for the ocean that he believed he couldn't live away from it for any length of time. From the time he started writing poetry, he devoted his time to capturing the romance and history of the sea and the Jersey Shore through poetry and sharing it with people in all parts of the world.

Cape May

From the time Andrea vacationed in Cape May and Cape May Point, he was completely taken by its charm. The "tips of the islands" always lured his poetic mind. He described Cape May and Cape May Point as "sea coast treasures": Full of history, beauty and the surrounding sea. He was intrigued by everything from the legacy of Henry Hudson and its colonization, to Cape May's Victorian beauty, which Andrea thought resembled the Island of Samoa in the South Pacific, the home of Robert Louis Stevenson. This coastal region possessed all the qualities Andrea needed to inspire him, and he ultimately made it his permanent home in 1954.

From the moment he settled in Cape May Point, he "got involved", embracing the town's history and supporting its advancement. He became involved in politics and charities, always having the good of Cape May at heart. He fought for such things as the preservation of its beaches, citizen property rights and the success and progress of its tourist industry, to name only a few. Andrea helped Cape May in times of trouble and eagerly promoted it on its most joyous occasions. He felt it was his destiny to do what he could for society at large and for the town he lived in.

Andrea had many passions in his life and involved himself with many causes and good deeds, and his hometown was no exception. Using tools he felt were given to him by God, of words, rhyme and perseverance, his goal was to make a difference. And that he did.

In June of 1999, Andrea was honored by the City of Cape May for his loyalty and his positive influence. He was recognized for his efforts and was given a proclamation by Mayor Robert Elwell. The moving words in the proclamation give just a glimpse of Andrea's devotion and love for the city:

PROCLAMATION
Dr. Andrea Lippi

WHEREAS, Dr. Andrea Lippi has lived in the Cape May area for many years and

WHEREAS, he has distinguished himself by carrying the name of Cape May City wherever he goes internationally and telling of its attributes and

WHEREAS, when he travels around the world he has become Cape May's International Ambassador and

WHEREAS, he has a great interest in Cape May's beach problems and he has always promoted for beach funding and

WHEREAS, he has always shared his God given talents without thought of remuneration,

NOW THEREFORE, BE IT RESOLVED, that I, Robert W. Elwell, Sr., Mayor of the City of Cape May, do hereby proclaim Dr. Andrea Lippi as Poet Laureate and International Ambassador for the City of Cape May.

IN WITNESS THEREOF, I have hereunto set my hand and caused the seal of the City of Cape May to be affixed this 15th day of June, 1999.

Attest:

Virginia E. Petersen

Virginia E. Peterson
City Clerk

Robert W. Elwell

Robert W. Elwell, Sr.
Mayor

Moved by the honor, Andrea said in an interview that day, "In all fairness, the ability I have been given to do the things I have been able to do over a long period of years and to write my poems, have come to me from the Great Lord in heaven. I feel I am sent to do this as the work of my life and feel Cape May is my chosen city."

In some of Andrea's poetry, he portrays Cape May as an inviting and welcoming city. Published in papers all over the world, these poems were meant to entice the reader, telling of its splendor and glory:

Spend The Day In Old Cape May

What better place to spend the day
Than by the bay in old Cape May

Watch the boats as they sail by
Listen to the seagulls cry.

Make believe the world is yours,
Cast a line with those magic lures.

Take a snooze let the world roll by
Consider yourself a lucky guy

When you are in Cape May.

Cape May Train

Take the train to Cape May
And to the State Park too
Take the train to Cape May
Stop by and see the zoo

We will all have a party
So let's not be tardy
Spend a wonderful day
Take the train to Cape May

Take the train to Cape May
Stop by and see the beach
Sand and the ballpark
Is all in easy reach

You can visit the Light House
All have dinner at my house
Spend a wonderful day
Take the train to Cape May

On the city's 350th Anniversary in 1959, Andrea became a part of the celebration committee and involved himself with many different projects. One such venture was promoting the coming of the Half Moon, a replica of Henry Hudson's famous ship. Hudson is the first western explorer credited with identifying the Cape May peninsula in 1609 while on a voyage to find passage through North America to the East Indies.

The replica, operated by the Netherlands Museum in North Carolina, was 100 feet long and featured a 12-man crew in period clothes who doubled as tour guides. This ship made many stops at different ports in America, and it was brought to Cape May to commemorate its anniversary. Andrea, a lover of history, the sea and exploration, wrote a heartfelt poem for the event, and everyone attending had a wonderful day.

The Immortal Henry Hudson

Set adrift in a ship's boat
On a treacherous icy sea
Henry Hudson and his loyal men
Victims of mutiny

No northern route to rich Cathay
Or the magic isles of Spice
Yet, discovered Hudson Bay
Almost touching the pole of ice

With his trusty ship the Half Moon
He discovered what is now Cape May
Watered his ship at a lovely lake
An earshot from Delaware Bay

Traded with the Indians
Enjoyed the summer sun
Bravo, Brave Captain Hudson
The final battle You have won;

Immortality.

A. Lippi

An Ode to Cape May County

Gem of four rich seasons
Cape May County great,
Bordered on the bay and the ocean
In the beautiful Garden State.

Settled by Henry Hudson,
Founded by courageous men,
Mariners see your lighthouse
Time and time again.

You're sure to find all beauty
Of the land, the sea and the sky,
So cherish Cape May County
Where the friendly seabirds fly.

An Ode To The Cape May Canal

Cape May gave its all
And answered the call

That men could be free
From the havoc of the sea

U-boats stalked our very shores
Battered with rams at our very doors

Murdered and maimed our men of the sea
Attempted to destroy the land of the free

But a canal was built that saved the day
With safety, our ships sailed their way

On March 2, 1962, the Jersey Coast was hit with a nor'easter, and Cape May Point suffered severe damages. As the Civil Defense Director for the Borough of Cape May Point, Andrea assisted in evaluating the damages and preparing the data for the Federal, State and County Authorities.

Andrea was inspired to start writing this poem in the middle of the night during the storm:

The sea rose up one mad March night
Battered the coast with all its might
Tide and waves frowned with scorn
Buildings wished they were never born.

No one remembers the sea so wild
Neptune himself was really riled
His trident pierced the land
Inlets created by his magic hand.

Storm was over and men looked around
It was sand that covered the once green ground.
So remember the story and the time of year
The ocean's wrath is a power to fear.

Andrea, a devout supporter of St. Mary's Convent in Cape May Point, was instrumental in getting beach protection underway to stabilize the beach and protect the historic landmark.

From left: The late NJ Senator Robert Kay, the Mother Superior of St. Mary's Convent, Mayor Michael Chomiak and Andrea Lippi.

For many years, Cape May had a problem with saltwater affecting its water supply. By 1995, it reached the point where something had to be done. All of the options were explored, and Cape May decided to construct the first desalination plant in the Northeast United States, which took the salty water and made it drinkable. It was a long-term solution for a long-standing problem. Two years worth of planning and building paid off for the city as it now has an assured water supply for the future.

Andrea presenting his poem of the desalination to Cape May Mayor, Thomas Phelan, who was Chairman of the Desalination Committee.

In an effort to inform and excite the citizens of Cape May, Andrea marked the event with this poem:

Desalination Cape May, USA

Desalination
Is the order Of the day

First in the Northeast
Historic Cape May

There is water everywhere
Bay and ocean plenty to spare

But drinking water may be in short supply
That is why Desalination is nigh.

A. Lippi

Captain Lippi's Light

I envisioned a lighthouse
So straight and so strong
Caressed by the winds
Where the sea sang its song.

Adorned by the sun
Enslaved by the moon
To all in its midst
It lamented his tune.

A poet came by
And wished there would be
A light on the beach
Where the land meets the sea.

A light on the beach
Where the days go astray
A vision of awe
In old South Cape May.

Andrea's love for oceanography led him to monitoring the Delaware Bay estuary for pollution. "I have done this for the last 17 years," Andrea said in an interview, "…accumulating tidal data, measuring the currents, and testing for mercury, sulfur, oil, industrial dyes and biological and industrial wastes." He did this out of concern for the coast, which gave him so much pleasure.

This led him to becoming founder of the Oceanographic Institute of Marine Sciences in Cape May County. It dealt with such issues as beach erosion and funding for shore protection, to name only a few.

The Institute cooperated with Millersville University to allow students to study the sea at the institute and receive credits for their courses. Andrea said, "The future looks even brighter for more education of the sea, and this will also help to combat pollution".

Andrea is seen showing his project to members of the Congressional Sub-Committee on Oceanography. From left: US Rep. James Saxton, Hon. Michael Lowery of Washington, DC and chairman of the Merchant Marine and Fisheries Committee on Oceanography and US Rep. William Hughes, a member of the Sub-Committee, who pledged his help for the success of Lippi's project. Background picture: Andrea with Dr. G. Alfred Forsyth, VP for Academic Affairs at the Millersville University congratulating him on their pioneering work on Oceanography along the Jersey Coast.

The Poet was travel editor and director of Public Relations for the 1966-1967 Second Edition of The New Jersey Almanac and Travel Guide. The book was "a comprehensive reference on New Jersey; for those who would know more about its industries, commerce, history, government, human and natural resources and other subjects relating to its civic, social, economic, educational and cultural development".

Andrea's poem, "An Ode To New Jersey", was published in the Almanac:

Along the Delaware and the Hudson
From ocean beaches to mountain high,
In a Mecca of earthly beauty
Does the State of New Jersey lie.
A heritage rich in history
Forefathers patriots true,
WITH PEOPLE, PURPOSE AND PROGRESS
May God send us blessings anew.

Gov. Richard J. Hughes of NJ was
presented with the special poem.

Senator Clifford Case, left and Senator Harrison Williams on right.

Andrea had a special place in his heart for Mayor Jack Vasser of West Cape May, New Jersey. Mayor Vasser was a very popular long-time mayor for the district. Like Andrea, he worked towards the success and development of Cape May County. He was known as "The People's Mayor" and was instrumental in appointing Andrea as Storm Center Research Reporter for the borough of West Cape May in 1985.

An Ode To Mayor Jack Vasser
(West Cape May)

The Stanley Steamer they built no more
Nor do they build the Model A
Take a look at Happy Jack Vasser
He is surely here to stay

Farmer, Patriot, Friend to all
Always ready to answer the call
Mayor of elegance and a gentleman too
Always ready to help me and you

When a historic shipwreck unveiled itself in 1954 in Cape May Point, Andrea quickly rushed to the site.

In the picture below, Andrea is seen with Freeholder Dr. Leon Schuck, a member of the County Historical Society. Andrea is pointing out specific markings identifying the wrecked boat as the British sloop Martin, which was sunk in the War of 1812.

It is currently housed under a wooden canopy with a stone monument telling the ship's tale:

"The British sloop of war HMS Martin which blockaded Delaware Bay in the War of 1812, was attacked, driven to the shoals, grounded and burned in 1813. Exposed by Hurricane Hazel in 1954 on Lighthouse Avenue in Cape May Point, she was salvaged, mounted, and placed on public display."

Andrea wrote many poems depicting the beauty of Cape May. This picturesque seashore resort held for him an oasis of ambiance and history. In an interview he gave many years ago, Andrea describes the romance and lure Cape May had for him. "The fishing docks, sand dunes, lovely old mansions, beautiful churches and houses of worship, the Cape May Country Store and the Lighthouse at the Point, these are all part of our beloved America – America the beautiful," he said. "Rich in history, Cape May County represents a great sea-faring heritage that should be cherished and perpetuated for the benefit of generations to come."

In Andrea's poems of Cape May, one can see he embraced all aspects of the region, from the smallest stone to the largest ocean.

Gem of the Jersey Coast

Beautiful Cape May City,
Gem of the Jersey Coast.
Treasure by the Ocean,
Place folks love the most.

Rich in American history,
A gift from God above.
Beautiful Cape May City,
The City the Sea does love.

Immortal Atlantis

Behold Atlantis
South Cape May
Once more you greet
The light of day

Once more you sleep
'Neath twinkling stars
Kissed by Venus
Adorned by Mars

Your mystic pyramid
Made of gold
Where magic miracles
Do unfold

Beckoning mortals
Young and old
Of your return
Were the prophets told

❧ The Legend of the Jersey Devil ❧

An old Scottish prayer reads, "From ghoulies and ghosties and long-leggetie beasties and things that go bump in the night, good Lord, deliver us!" This avid plea stays true for New Jersey as well, for it has its own legend of a creature that lurks in the pinelands of South Jersey. Andrea became quite intrigued with the folklore of The Jersey Devil.

There are many versions of the story, sometimes called "Leeds' Devil", but they all revolve around the birth of a child. The most common folktale is that The Jersey Devil is the offspring of one Mrs. Deborah Leeds from South Jersey, who, in 1735, after hearing she was pregnant with her 13th child, cursed it to be a devil. The child was born normal, but then changed from a baby to a creature with hooves, horns, a forked tail, bat wings, and a horse-like head. Upon changing, the creature flew up the chimney and out to the pinelands and has been scaring people ever since.

Andrea found the fable's history and documented sightings fascinating and wrote two poems telling of its tale. When he would visit different schools around the area, he would tell the children of The Jersey Devil and its folklore.

This next poem was included in a documentary film produced by Jersey State Television. Andrea lured the camera by reading his poem and talking of his own personal sighting of The Jersey Devil.

This etching of the Jersey (Leeds) Devil was created especially for Andrea by his artist friend, Mr. Ed Sheetz.

Leeds Devil

Deep in the marshes Leeds' devil is lurking
In the mist and the darkness he always is working.
Folks know his habits, haunts and devices.
Best guard yourself for the devil entices.
Down near the point where the reeds are highest
That's where the devil conjures the slyest.
Nights after dark, when the wind's off the ocean,
Best guard yourself lest he get a notion
And pounce upon you with pitchfork and saber
Rest of your life you'll be vexed by hard labor.
Now you've been warned; look out for Black Magic
To laugh or scoff will prove very tragic.
Jersey's the land the devil does roam,
Leeds' Point is the place he sits on his throne.

The Jolly Jersey Devil

The Jolly Jersey Devil
Is a friend of mine, you know,
And in the fairest Garden State,
I see him when I go.
In marshes by the river,
On the Boardwalk by the sea,
There on Trenton's stately streets,
He is proud as he can be.
The "Golden Dome" belongs to him,
Though the woods he calls his home,
The byways and the beaches
Are the places he will roam.
In legends and in stories,
He's a prankish sort of guy,
The "Jolly Jersey Devil'
Has a twinkle in his eye.

Longport

Longport, New Jersey held a special place in Andrea's heart because it was the place of his family's vacation home. Andrea spent much of his childhood there, by the sea, when the family wanted to escape the hustle and bustle of Philadelphia.

Perhaps Longport influenced Andrea's boyhood dreams of oceans and explorers, travel and distant lands.

Beloved Longport

Beloved Longport
How you have changed
You and I are
So estranged

Yet I think of you
Everyday
Fondest memories
Come my way

Many poems
For you I have penned
Something that
Will never end

Whether near
Or oh so far
You will always be
My shining star

Andrea wrote a poem recalling an actual childhood memory:

Longport By The Sea

We were driving South on Bay Street
In Longport by the sea
We were in a Model A
Proud as we could be.

It was 4th of July in the morning
Just about 10am
We had loads of fireworks in the back seat
Celebrating was our aim.

We were throwing them out the window
As we were driving along
One by one they flew through the air
Whistling and singing their song.

One firecracker got in the crate
Then they all started to go
They exploded like a volcano
And that put on quite a show.

The back seat was shattered
But we didn't give a hoot
The people looking from the curb
Thought the deal was cute.

A. Lippi

An Ode To Lovetts' – at Longport Bridge

(Lovetts was a famous boatyard)

Lovetts' yard
Knows no change.
And if it would,
It would be quite strange.

Pillard – Coppage –Lampson
And all –
Still hang around
Have a ball

Gramps and Dick
Are always there
Can't get away
From that Longport air

A part of the world
A special place
Hallmark of Chris Craft
Lovetts' place.

Andrea posing for a picture with Mr. Lovett
and friend, John Wanamaker.

On September 10 of 1990, Longport's new long-awaited county library was opening its doors. At the ribbon cutting ceremony, Andrea was there to dedicate a poem to his boyhood town:

Longport Library

Longport, Child of the sea and sand
Truly an enchanted land
By a bay beside the sea
Steep in joy and memory

Today we are here to dedicate a building
Standing at the gate of knowledge
Art and wisdom rare
A monument in the crisp sea air

Where minds can grow
And men may find
A truly inward
Peace of mind

Where books are king
And thoughts are great
For this moment,
Did the Angels wait.

⤜ *Lucy the Elephant* ⤛

The beach town of Margate is directly next to Longport, and, it is safe to say, Andrea grew up knowing Lucy the Elephant.

In 1881, the 65-foot tall sculpture was built as a real estate attraction but later held the titles of hotel, private beach cottage, tavern and tourist attraction. After years of neglect, she was renovated in 1970 and is listed on the National Register of Historic Places.

Anyone driving up and down the main road along the coast would gaze at the landmark with a smile. Andrea wrote two poems honoring Lucy, a childhood memory:

Lucy – the Margate Elephant
I live beside the sea.

The children – all the time
Come and visit me.

I tell them tales of long ago
And things that happen now

A whale that walked upon the beach
I thought she was a cow.

The moon one night when he was full
He whispered in my ear

"Lucy, won't you marry me?
For you my love is clear."

I just smiled and winked my eye
And in my girlish way

Said, "Moon, it's better we not wed –
Let's spend our time at play."

Ode To Lucy - The Margate Elephant

Lucy, dear Lucy,
A friend once so gay,
Alone on the beach
Just wasting away.

Storms have defaced her
But not touched her soul;
'Neath her sheet metal hide
Beats a heart of pure gold.

Once lodging and food,
She supplied with great pride.
Her owners gone,
Cast her aside.

Dear Elephant Lady
The time on her rides,
Are there not some kind souls
That will take her in stride?

To paint her and fix her,
To cherish her name,
With her hide, oh, so bright
She will gain all her fame.

To be saved now forever
Her song they will sing,
In the hearts of the young
Her legend will ring.

Lucy, dear Lucy
A friend now so gay
She brightens our paths
As we pass by her way.

When visiting different coastlines in his travels, Andrea was inspired to write poetry for the beautiful coastal towns of Ocean City and Sea Isle City:

All Aboard for Ocean City

All aboard for Ocean City,
Twenty-five cents they would say

Cast the line and turn the wheel,
As the accordion man does play

His kazoo and his washboard,
Made the seagulls scamp and play

As "The Collins" and "The Colonel"
Went along their chosen way.

Times have changed the boats are gone
But in Heaven you can hear them say;

All aboard for Ocean City
It's a nice trip across the bay.

An Ode to Sea Isle City

The heavens smile on Sea Isle,
City by the sea.
Great place for vacations,
Where time goes merrily.

Spacious sandy beaches,
Harbors and lagoons.
Pathways by the ocean,
Where the winds sing happy tunes.

Fishing at its finest,
Bathing at its best!
So come on down to Sea Isle,
Where we say, BE MY GUEST!

*A*ndrea Lippi was a visionary man who foresaw Cape May to be the charming city that it is today.   A hopeless romantic, he thought that enchanting gaslights would be the perfect adornment for Cape May's growing Victorian Village on Washington Street.   And as chance had it…. he knew exactly where to get some.

Philadelphia had pulled up their city's gaslights a few years prior to update to new modern methods. They were put up for sale, and Andrea purchased 13 of them from the Philadelphia Street Department for a mere $37.50 each.

After moving to Cape May, Andrea envisioned his gaslights standing proudly in a prominent place in the town. In 1959, he sold 12 of them to the city for the purchase price plus the cost to electrify them. The city of Cape May appointed Andrea Chairman of the gaslight committee, and off he went to make the installation happen in time for Cape May's 350th Anniversary Celebration, which was right around the corner.

In a letter to the mayor, Andrea wrote, "…. the installation of these gaslights on the business blocks of Washington Street will be a great asset to the undisputed charm of historic and beautiful Cape May". He assured the city that the merchants were very excited about the idea and would be more than pleased to pay the cost of the electrified lamps.

With plans officially under way for the installation, it was now Andrea's job to raise awareness and excitement. What better way to do that than with poems and tales.

Harold E. Mason, left, Philadelphia street lighting engineer, formally transfers the gas lights to the City of Cape May, represented by Andrea and Mayor Carl R. Youngberg.

Arrival of the gaslights.

Andrea wrote a poem to commemorate the arrival of the Philadelphia gaslights:

Friendly Light

Oh friendly light, you served so well
What wondrous stories you can tell.
Now for your work to all mankind
Bright new pastures you do find.

To far off cities you will go
To spread your friendly guiding glow.
Philadelphia has set you free
Now all the world you will see.

Installation of the gaslights.

No words can best describe Andrea's passion for the gaslights better than his very own. He wrote a most endearing story, his own romantic version, of the gaslights coming to Cape May. This was published on May 28th, 1959 in the Cape May County News:

Many years ago in Colonial Philadelphia before the time of electricity, gaslight illuminated the city streets and held a position of great esteem. Yes, they saw all the happenings of the day and night and would discuss these things among themselves, being careful not to let the neighbors or passersby hear them.

They were discussing the summer vacation resorts one spring night after seeing the Jones Family pack up their trunks and baggage, shut up the house and leave for the long summer vacation at Cape May. In those days the vacationers would sail down the Delaware on the steamer Republic.

The gaslight that stood in front of the Jones' house said with a sigh, "Oh, how I wish I could go to lovely Cape May someday".

The light across the street whispered, "Just keep wishing and maybe an angel will grant your wish someday".

Many, many years passed and new people moved in and out of the Jones' house, but the faithful gaslight each night would say a prayer to the angel wishing to go to Cape May.

The old lamplighter knew this good lamp very well and would sing a lullaby to the little light and would caress it as he lit its light.

Modern day came to Philadelphia, and the lamp lights knew their day was done. They would laugh at the light that wanted to go to Cape May, saying, "Little light, you know where you are going".

But the little light prayed and prayed.

Then one day, men came along the street and took up all the gaslights and sent them to a yard. The other lights cried but the little light prayed and prayed.

Then a strange thing happened. The man who owned the lights got a phone call from Cape May, asking him about the lights, and ordering 12 to be sent to Cape May City. All the lights heard the news and began to pray themselves. The yard man walked right over to the little light and wrote with yellow chalk in big letters, CAPE MAY, N.J.

The little light's prayers were answered.

We all bid the lights welcome to Cape May and know that he who has the faith of a mustard seed can move mountains. For faith brought the lights to Cape May.

This story was published again on July 2, 1959 at the request of many. The city loved it. Coincidentally, the gaslights were being set up on Washington Street in Cape May that week.

Many more gaslights have been purchased for Cape May since 1959, but all who were there at the 350th Anniversary recall the joy of seeing the first gaslights standing proud and tall at the Washington Street Mall.

Gaslights and Tulips

Gaslights and tulips
Memories young and old
Tales to remember
That history does unfold

Captain Mey "Cornelius"
From the Netherlands did sail
The Indians gazed upon his ship
As though it were a whale

New Port May was founded
And added to the chart
Today we know its beauty
Its buildings works of art

Its harbors and its beaches
Its meadows and its light
All endowed by heaven
To afford man's rare delight

Andrea held on to his remaining gaslight for years. He felt that it would have an appropriate home in Hoorn, Holland, which was the birthplace of Captain Cornelius Mey, founder of Cape May.

In 1981, on behalf of the city as Good Will Ambassador of Cape May, Andrea paid a special visit to Holland. He presented the gaslight to the people of Hoorn, together with a proclamation from the city of Cape May, New Jersey signed by Mayor Arthur Blomkvest, pledging friendship between the two cities. He called them "sister cities".

Andrea said that, "the townsfolk in Hoorn were most courteous, and they received the gaslight with fine enthusiasm." He asked for it to be installed in the Dutch city to remind citizens of their Cape May friends.

A poem was written for this special occasion and Andrea was most proud to reacquaint the cities and show respect to the hometown of a Dutch man, who, like Andrea, foresaw Cape May.

Andrea presenting a 'proclamation of friendship' from the City of Cape May and a gas light to Lord Mayor Janssens of the City of Hoorn, Holland.

Off to Hoorn

Off to Hoorn, with a gaslight
To honor Captain Mey.
Off to Hoorn with a gaslight
To spend a happy day.

To Friesland where the happy folk
Say "Welcome" with a smile.
'tis there, the Cape May gaslight
Plans to spend awhile.

So when eventide approaches
The gaslight starts to glow.
Across the great Atlantic
The gaslight says "Hello."

$\mathcal{C}$aptain Lippi had a passion for ships. Any ship. Even sinking ships. And there was such a vessel in his hometown: The famous Concrete Ship.

Since 1926, just off of Sunset Beach at the Cape May Point, a concrete ship called the SS Atlantus lies to rest. Due to a critical shortage of steel during WWI, the Federal Government commissioned 38 ships to be built using other material. Using an experimental design patented by a Norwegian inventor in 1912, concrete was used to make the hull. Only 12 ships were ever completed and put to service.

A. Lippi

The Atlantus was built by the Liberty Shipbuilding Corporation of Brunswick, Georgia. The freighter weighed 3,000 tons and was 250 feet long with a six-inch thick hull made of special concrete aggregate. She was launched on November 21, 1918 from Wilmington, North Carolina. On June 1, 1919, the Atlantus was commissioned to serve for a year as a government-owned privately operated commercial coal steamer in New England.

At the end of the war, the more efficient steel ships were again available, and the Concrete Fleet was de-commissioned because they became too expensive to operate. Their heavy hull needed too much fuel to push them around, and so the ships became obsolete. In September of 1920, the "Atlantus" was sent to the "Bone Yard" at "Pigs Point" in Norfolk, Virginia. A year later she was purchased by a salvage company and stripped.

In 1926, the Atlantus was purchased and towed to Cape May. A Baltimore firm was attempting to start a ferry service from Cape May to Lewes, Delaware and wanted to use the ship as part of a dock on the proposed ferry line. While the ship was anchored near the site, awaiting its fate, a storm hit the region and the ship broke loose and grounded itself off of Sunset Beach in Cape May Point. Stuck fast in the sand, all attempts to move it failed. The vessel found its final resting place.

And so the Atlantus sat at Cape May Point where locals fished from her dock and hung advertising banners on her hull. Rumor had it that it was used to store smuggled whiskey during Prohibition. Andrea Lippi felt all this was "an insult to all once-proud ships", and in 1957, started a movement to have the advertising signs removed and have the name Atlantus restored to the hull.

Knowing it was only a matter of time that the ship would eventually be completely under water, Andrea was very passionate about returning some dignity to the ship and wrote a poem to try and do just that:

Vanishing Ship

Concrete ship
May one day
Be no more

Its stony hull
Resting on the
Ocean floor

But oh what
Memories
Will prevail

It withstood
The storm
And gale

But now time
Has had its
Way

The ship has
Seen its
Better day

But its memory
Will linger
Yeah for sure

For its all
A part
Of Cape May lure

Because the SS Atlantus was the most famous of the concrete ships made during the war, it became quite a landmark for the residents and an attraction for the visitors. Busloads of children would come on field trips to view the ship. Many photos were taken at the Point, and, because the ship was steadily sinking, snapshots were different from one year to the next. For years, the spectacular sunsets of the Point were always viewed with the ship in its setting. Today, the tide only occasionally allows a small peak of the vessel, which will soon remain hidden away, out of sight, but nonetheless, still "...a part of Cape May lure".

*T*he first car to cross the Delaware Bay on the new ferry between Cape May and Lewes, Delaware on its first sailing was, none other than, Andrea Lippi's.

Delaware and Cape May both proposed to join the two states with a ferry back in 1958. The idea was to make South Jersey accessible to both commercial and tourist interests on both sides of the Delaware Bay without the long drive. Andrea's love of the sea and sailing drew him straight to the project. During the pertinent years of planning the ferry, Andrea was the publicity and promotional director for the Cape May Chamber of Commerce. He worked with government and business interests from both states to bring the project to fruition.

Andrea would often meet with the citizens of Cape May to discuss the ferry and its positive potential for the city. "The time has come for the business people of Cape May County to take the destiny of their city in their hands."

Andrea felt so strongly about the ferry and its promising success, he promoted it the best way he knew how... he wrote a poem:

Delaware Ferry

Delaware and New Jersey
Have signed a pact they say
An agreement to start a ferry
Crossing Delaware Bay

Governors Hughes and Carvel
Are men of enormous zeal
The ferries may ply both north and south
To aid the automobile

Trucks and loaded trailers
Will go their chosen way
Progress is here to greet us
Prosperity is here to stay

Thank God for the Bay and River
In Delaware Valley great
Bless the busy ferry boat
When it sails from state to state.

Andrea presented this poem at the December 1962 meeting after a "trial ferry run".

At a meeting with Delaware citizens: From left - Milt Fried, editor of the Delaware Coast Press; Winfield Brittingham, head of the Waterways Committee of Lewes; Fred Karl, president of the Rehoboth Beach Chamber of Commerce; Juel C. Stamper, Mayor of Rehoboth Beach; Andrea Lippi; Frank Robinson, president of the Lewes Chamber of Commerce; and Frank Buck, City Manager of Rehoboth Beach.

From Left: G Winifred Brittingham, head of the Delaware Waterways Committee; Frank Robingson of Lewes; Freeholder Edwin Zaberer of Cape May County and Andrea Lippi at the Cape Island Marina Inn at the trial ferry run.

And so on July 1, 1964, Andrea Lippi arrived at the Cape May terminal at 3:00 a.m. and spent the night in his brand new black 1964 1/2 Ford Mustang. The car was built especially for Andrea at the request of Henry Ford, and he drove it 'off the lot' from a Michigan dealership only days before the sail. Andrea drove the car all the way to New Jersey to be the first one waiting when the ferry doors opened. He was determined to be the first passenger aboard the vessel. "It looked like Dunkirk," he said referring to the famous WWII battle at the French seaport. "There was nobody there at all when I got there. There was just a dirt road that led up to a little shack and a makeshift ramp to get cars onto the ferry. It was eerie," Andrea remembered years later with vivid recollection.

A. Lippi

Andrea purchased the first two tickets for the 'car and passenger' fare and the 1ˢᵗ foot passenger ticket. The *firsts*, he saved for souvenirs and the 2ⁿᵈ he used to board the ferry. At 6:40 a.m., it carried seven vehicles, a mobile trailer and 26 passengers on the 17-mile run to Delaware.

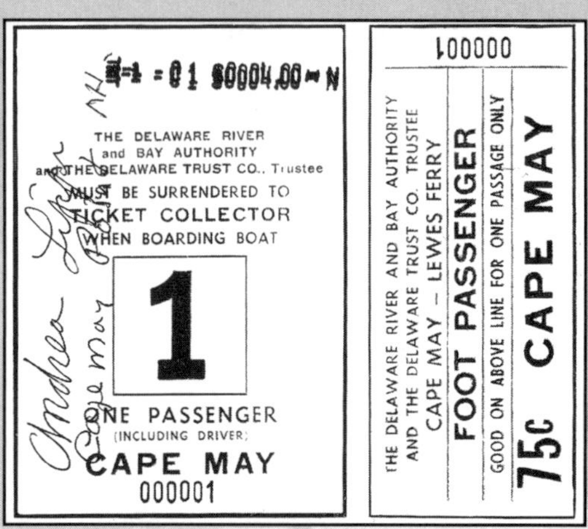

When new vessels were purchased for the ferry line, Andrea would be there to celebrate the Christening. The vessels would grow in technology and sophistication and shorten in sailing time. By the time the fifth vessel was purchased in 1989, it took only 70 minutes to go from state to state.

In 1985, Andrea is showing Joseph Haggerty the first ticket sold for the Cape May-Lewes ferry. Haggerty sold Lippi the ticket over 20 years prior.

On the 25th Anniversary of the ferry in 1989, Andrea and other "first-ferry travelers" were invited back for its Silver Anniversary celebration. Mr. David Chapman, general manager of the ferry, called Andrea directly and asked him to play his part in the celebration to recreate the first ferry run. Mr. Chapman remembers Andrea fondly in the years he worked at the ferry. He said of Andrea, "In my 15 years, he was always a source of inspiration and had a wonderful gift of poetry and love for the ferry operation and the beauty of the bay it sailed on".

Andrea wrote a special poem commemorating the ferry's anniversary:

25 Years of Service

New Jersey and Delaware
Do celebrate today
25 years of service
Crossing Delaware Bay.

Linking Florida and New England
Then all the Eastern States.
A path across the waters
Where joy and leisure wait.

A jewel of a journey
A Blessing to be sure
Thank God for the bay and river
May the Ferry e'er endure.

At 6:30 a.m. on June 30, 1989, Andrea was, once again, the first passenger to board the ferry. He was driving a 1965 black Ford Mustang similar to the one he had at the first ferry ride. Andrea said he had been searching for the car for months prior to the anniversary date but had no success. A week prior to the event, he saw a red 1965 mustang parked on the side of the road on Rt. 47 in Cape May County. The car was not for sale, but Andrea made the owner an offer he couldn't refuse and drove away with the car. A rush paint job gave Andrea his black Mustang to proudly drive on the ferry and recreate what he had done 25 years earlier.

More than 17,000 people turned up for this milestone celebration, and it was a "perfect day". When Andrea stepped back on Cape May's shore after his trip, a reporter asked for his statement: "Marvelous," he said, and Andrea estimated that he had taken the ferry between 150 to 200 times in its 25 years of service.   Then he whipped out dozens of lines of sea-inspired poetry for the media that had gathered to greet him:

> *I like to sit*
>
> *And watch the ships*
>
> *That anchor in the bay.*
>
> *The ships that linger*
>
> *For a while*
>
> *But never ever stay.*

In 1990, Andrea and his wife made a "25 Plus One" crossing to relive the ferry's anniversary date.

26th Anniversary - Andrea is seen with, from left, David Chapman, ferry manager; Robert Conroy, Lower Township mayor and Robert Vance, ferry pilot.

A. Lippi

Andrea wrote a poem for the 1990 Anniversary:

The Ferry Boat

Highlight of the season
Was the ride across the bay
Aboard the lovely Ferry Boat
From Lewes to Cape May.

A '64 Ford Mustang
Was proud as it could be
To pose for the picture
That you can plainly see.

A camera took the photo
The papers used it too
Highlight of the season
A Poem from me to you.

On the ferry's 30th Anniversary, guess who was the first passenger on board? Andrea had with him his Mustang and a poem to celebrate the occasion:

30 years across the bay
Glad the ferry came our way.

Connecting Maine and Florida too
Get in your car and drive right through.

Shiny ships go their way
All to make for a happy day.

Cape May and Lewes, a place in the sun
Making travel easy and fun.

Andrea once said, "Whenever I have nothing to do, I get on the ferry and ride. I think I'm in Europe or the South Seas. A two hour ride on the ferry will ease anybody's mind."

$\mathcal{A}$ndrea devoted a large part of his life to sharing his experiences with people. With a tape recorder in one hand and a camera in the other, he interviewed, reported and made incredible photos of fascinating people and topics, chasing his passions along the way. Either on his radio show in Bridgeton, NJ, his TV show in Wildwood or numerous newsprint publications, Andrea always kept his audience entertained with stories, pictures, and of course, poetry.

He started his radio show in the 1950's, and it aired intermittently on various radio stations from Philadelphia to New Jersey to New York and places in between. His objective was to bring interesting topics to his audience; sharing the experiences of his travels and all he encountered on his search for a good cause and inspiration.

Andrea enjoyed this very much and felt blessed to be able to pursue what he loved. In an interview he said, "My life is a vacation – I just travel and write because my work is my life."

Andrea loved reciting his poems to a public audience. This was the perfect venue for him to share what he loved with anyone who would listen. He felt that each of his poems had a message for the listener but not one that needed to be searched for. Together with his poetry, he featured everything from local news and events, interviews with politicians, charitable causes, international travel and the list goes on and on.

Here we will share with you only a taste of Andrea's experiences and pleasures through pictures and poems:

PHOTO

More magic in a photo
Than you can ever know
Bringing back memories
Dreams of long ago
Reaching deep inside your soul
Transcending time and space
The magic in a photo
Nothing can replace

At a Warner Brothers Seven Arts Film Festival in Freeport, Bahamas, Andrea chatted with such big wigs as Ernest Borgnine (pictured), Danny Kaye, William Holden and Veronica Carson and presented his interviews on his "Captain Lippi Show".

In this rare photo taken in the 1950's, Andrea is seen with the family of the late Mario Lanza who were visiting in Wildwood, NJ at the time. The family agreed to be interviewed and was perfect for broadcasting on his radio show.

The interview was recorded at the home of Mario Lanza's grandfather, Salvatore Lanza, seen left of Andrea, where Mario spent many summers as a boy.

To the right of Andrea sits Mario's mother and seated below are his children, Damon, Ellisa, Marc and Colleen.

TEXAS

Take me back to Texas
To the rolling cattle land
Take me back to Texas
Put a six gun in my hand

Take me back to Texas
Where I'll never ever sigh
For when I stand on Texas soil
A mighty man am I

I'm a powerful man in Texas
For there I have my rights
There I drink my liquor
There I pick my fights

There I love my woman
And there I'm going to die
So take me back to Texas
Where I'll say my last GOOD BYE

Andrea wrote this fun poem for Texas, which he presented to President Lyndon B. Johnson and Lady Bird, who were Texans. Andrea was at the Waldorf Astoria hotel to greet the special guests attending a benefit by the Thomas A. Dooley Foundation.

While at the reception, Andrea interviewed Mrs. Agnes Dooley, mother of the late Dr. Dooley, for International Broadcasting. The interview was tape recorded for use on his radio program.

This wonderful picture was published in the Philadelphia Daily News in March of 1957. Andrea is seen here with the lovely Eva Gabor and Jerry Colonna. The trio came together at the Philadelphia Sheraton to kick off a drive for Hungarian Relief Funds.

In this darling picture, the famous Lassie assists Andrea, Publicity Director of the Sea Isle City Chamber, in presenting a plaque of Outstanding Service to H. Werner Buck.

Mr. Buck was president of Show Management, Inc., international trade show producers at the annual New York Sports, Travel and Vacation Show. The ceremony took place at the Coliseum in New York City with 5,000 spectators present.

This New York Show had a successful ten-day run, and Andrea would broadcast daily from the coliseum to radio stations throughout the United States.

In the first months of 1960, Kilanea volcano, near the easternmost point of the Hawaiian Islands, erupted with a vengeance. Andrea was there with microphone in hand, reporting on the conditions of the island. He recorded a radio broadcast tape for rebroadcast to a series of 70 readied radio programs.

Sadly, Andrea saw the Kapoho Village had been totally engulfed by lava and the Kumukahi lighthouse, less than ½ mile away, was also in the lava's path. The next day, however, planes reported that the steel tower stood tall. It was found that the lava split about 20 feet in front of the tower and swept within two yards of the tower itself on both sides as it headed toward the sea.

Andrea went and visited the site of the lighthouse shortly after the lava cooled and reported on its miraculous condition. He took with him an American Flag, which was flown over the structure just after the lava surrounded the area. This was to show support and respect for the wonder that occurred. The flag was then presented to Congressman Milton W. Glenn at a ceremony at Congress Hall in Cape May.

Cape Kumukahi lighthouse became a lava phenomenon, and the Hawaiians believed God spared the light, for the light surely had steered many sailors home. The lava was now sacred territory and should not be disturbed. According to Hawaiian legend, Pele, the volcano Goddess, protected the Hawaiian fisher folk by sparing the lighthouse. The Islanders believed they were sent a spiritual message with only the town's church and lighthouse untouched.

It is at this point that Andrea took a dedicated interest in the saga of the light on Kumukahi Point and it becomes more than a story of lava and volcanoes, but of a love of folklore and a coming together of a village.

When Andrea learned that the Coast Guard planned to cut through the lava to reinstate the road, he started a one-man campaign aimed at preserving the light and the ancient folklore instilled in the area.

He enlisted the support of Hawaii's Governor, Congressman and State Senator, to name a few. He asked assistance from his listeners to support building the road around the lighthouse instead of bulldozing through the lava.

With a poet's faith and a willingness to tackle a project of major proportions, Andrea shaped the course of the future for that Coast Guard lighthouse on Kumukahi Point.

So thus, the story ends with the U.S. Coast Guard lighthouse still standing tall, with the hardened lava skirting around the base and her beacon still shining out to sea.

Andrea was able to create quite a following with his radio program and, in 1967, started a weekly television program of great success that lasted 15 years. His TV show aired on WCMC in Wildwood, NJ (an NBC affiliate) and was periodically picked up in Philadelphia, Atlantic City and New York. In front of a camera, Andrea was a natural, charming his audience with stories and rhyme.

On the first anniversary of the Captain Lippi Show, Andrea celebrated his success in style! He held the celebration live surrounded by gorgeous models from the Le Jolie School. This brilliant photo created quite a buzz and was used in publications all over the world.

The year was 1970 and Andrea found himself handling publicity for the New York Mets. After winning the World Series in 1969 against the

Orioles, the players and their wives were treated to a two-week cruise of the Mediterranean. Andrea was chosen to handle publicity on the tour as well as file reports of the voyage back to the States. Andrea also collected films and taped interviews with the players and coaches on the trip for use on his show.

On the Captain Lippi TV Show, Andrea held a special Armistice Day program and a salute to veterans and all recruiting services. He brought together (left to right) Master Sgt. James Thomas, Area U.S. Army Recruiting Supervisor; Sgt. Kenneth Lewis, U.S. Marine Corps; POI William Johnston and CPO Dutch Holland U.S. Navy Recruiting Reps of Atlantic and Cape May Counties; Mr. Henry Matthews, Public Relations and Sales Rep, McCarthy Ford, Inc.; and Sgt. Thomas Peterson, U.S. Air Force recruiter.

Andrea highly supported the armed forces and believed in the power of serving one's country.

On one of Andrea's TV programs in the early 1970's, he had the joy of having his father-in-law as a special guest. Mr. Aloys Meesters from the Netherlands proudly presented Andrea with the latest record from the St. Cecilia Choir from the town of Vaals.

This choir, named for the saint of music, dates back to 1837 and still stands as the oldest choir in the province of Limburg. Its membership then was roughly 80 to 100 men.

The members of St. Cecilia were very dedicated and earned a lot of merit through the years with many talented voices. One of these voices belonged to Mr. Meesters, who sang Tenor for the choir for more than 60 years. He, along with his four brothers, was completely committed to St. Cecilia Choir for many years.

The St. Cecilia Choir preferred singing at philanthropic events and benefits for good deeds. They were quite sought after and sang all over Europe, including in the concert halls of Vienna, Antwerpen and Paris.

In the charming picture below, the choir is gathered at the Hotel Kasteel Bloemendal. The building was once a well-known French-speaking convent and school, the Sacre Coeur, in which Mrs. Rose Kennedy as well as other famous people, attended.

Andrea would periodically play the music sung by the St. Cecilia Choir on his show - much to the delight of his following - for whom he did everything.

Andrea just loved talking about Spain. It was one of his favorite places on earth, and he loved to talk about it on his radio and TV shows. He gathered stories and interviews there and even filmed a special show covering the ABTA Convention (Association of British Travel Agents) at the Congress Hall in Torremolinos.

With the pretty girls from the Malaga School who took part in the ABTA Convention.

Filming on the coast of Spain for his local TV show,
Andrea visits with young beachcombers.

In an interview he had in Spain the day he was leaving for the United States, Andrea told the reporter, "Spain is the home of my soul. I have spent hours on the beaches, around the ports…..writing, sketching and taking pictures." He continued, "Now I am off, back to put it all in my show." And that is exactly what he did….time and time again.

Andrea with those pretty Spanish girls again.

Andrea was blessed with good luck and perfect timing. A pleasant coincidence happened in Florida in the Spring of 1975 for both Andrea and Muhammad Ali. Ali, who was staying at the famous Hotel Fountainebleau, heard by chance of Andrea and his poetry. Being a writer of poetry himself, Ali was intrigued and invited Andrea to his suite. Next thing they knew, they were fascinated with each other's poetry and were swapping poems.

What a wonderful story to be shared on his television show.

Andrea was fascinated with England's majestic Ocean Liner, the QE II. When the ship was to visit Philadelphia on April 25, 1982 to commemorate her 300th birthday, Andrea was, of course, on hand to meet the ship, which sailed up the Delaware, docking at Philadelphia's port.

For this premier voyage to Philadelphia, the ship was named *The Welcome*, which was the name of the ship that first brought William Penn to this country. As the QE II was docking, Andrea was at a vantage point atop a hotel on a Trans-Atlantic telephone hookup to the BBC Bush House and the United Press International in London. He provided British radio listeners with a first-person description of the docking of the ship and the celebration surrounding the event as it was happening. Immediately after the reports to England, Andrea did a series of reports to WCMC Wildwood-by-the-Sea, covering the events of the day.

Andrea hosted a cocktail party following the arrival for members of the press and foreign dignitaries. The poet was honored when the ship's skipper, Capt. Alexander Hutchinson, formally accepted a framed print of Andrea's poem commemorating the historic docking and the history of the voyage.

PHILADELPHIA IS PROUD
To welcome the "Welcome" QE II

Philadelphia is proud and pleased
To welcome the "Welcome"
A Queen of the Seas,
The QE II, is here this day
To extol: *The American Way.*

William Penn 300 years ago
Sailed to our shores
That the world might know
That freedom is man's given right.
He was led by God
And a guiding light.

Today what we see
Is a spectacle great –
PHILADELPHIA'S BIRTHDAY
Let's celebrate!

-Andrea Lippi

Written especially for the Queen Elizabeth II
Visit on Philadelphia's 300th Birthday.

This poem was also inspired by the QE II coming to Philadelphia:

An Ode To Britannia and the QEII

From the Falklands back to Dover,
Rings an echo loud and clear.

The British marines have landed
And the QE II is here.

The Union Jack is waving
O'er The Islands, to be sure.

The Navy and the Air Force
Flash a message — "All Secure."

Back in London they are saying:
"Praise the Lord and Save the Queen."

O'er the oceans men are saying,
"Yes, Britannia reigns supreme."

Andrea collected his inspiration in the form of pictures of people and places, taped recordings and motion picture film, and he was grateful for every minute of it. Andrea was a very religious man, and every evening after his show, he ended with a prayer:

Oh Lord,
May I be a better person tomorrow than I was today
May I enjoy my work as I enjoy my play
May I thank you for tomorrow as I thank you for today

*A*ndrea Lippi adored traveling. He would pick up and go in a minute, for it inspired him. His visiting different places made him an explorer, while finding a quest and a passion, created a poem. He traveled extensively, and whether in Europe, the Middle East, the South Seas or the US, found inspiration and positive energy from the beauty of the places he visited and from finding an occasion for a poem.

In nearly all he did, he would act as a sort of Ambassador for the Jersey Cape, talking of its beauty and sharing his poetry. Whether traveling for his TV or Radio Shows or to simply deliver a poem, his magnetic character would draw a crowd. All of Andrea's travels couldn't possibly be listed in this book, but we will mention his favorites and the ones most special to him.

A. Lippi

Lord When We Travel

Lord when we travel
Look after our needs

Lord when we travel
Be pleased with our deeds

Lord when we travel
May your wonders we find

Lord when we travel
We ask your help divine

England

Andrea loved England and visited many times. He wrote a poem of the magnificent Tower Bridge of London and, on one of his trips, presented it to the manager of the Tower Bridge Hotel, as seen in the wonderful picture below.

From Tower Bridge To Tilbury

From Tower Bridge to Tilbury
Along the River Thames,
Are ships and docks and derricks high
Where commerce never ends.

A river of tradition
Where Kings and Queens were born,
Naturally it runs
Quite true to form.

Its fame will be undying
A password of the sea –
Thames and the Pool London
A wondrous sight to be

London is a city with many fountains and sculptures sometimes used to promote a particular place, as well as beautify the area. The fountain beside the Tower Bridge, created by the famous David Wynne, was unveiled in 1973 by Lord Aldington, Chairman of the Port of London Authority. He hoped the sculpture would symbolize the re-awakening of the site of the Hospice of Saint Katharine-by-the-Tower.

Andrea was enchanted with the sculpture and wrote this poem:

Girl With A Dolphin

Girl with a dolphin "In London Town"
'Neath Tower Bridge does play
While river ducks look down and smile
And ships in Harbour say:

"Good dolphin be ye oh so blessed
To have a friend so rare"
Then frisk and play 'neath sun and stars
As the Thames flows off its cares

Great London does play host to muses
As the world puts on its play
The girl with the dolphin in a poem.
Go merrily on their way.

Poem of the Sea
For the Queen's Jubilee

England and ships go,
With great harmony;
Melville and Cook, Hudson and Nelson
– Men of the sea.

From crosstrees to keelson,
The pen and the sword, the wheel and the sail
The sun and the stars
The wind and the gale.

The dream and the voyage
The bright summer's day
The Thames and the Clyde
Each go their way.

England for sure,
the Oceans do know –
Her Majesty's Ships
O'er the sea ever go.

Holland

Andrea visited Holland many times, and one particular town was favored in his heart, for it was the homeland of his wife, Catherine. Vaals, in the Province of Limburg, lies at the highest point of the Netherlands, which is 323 meters above sea level. But its most remarkable point is the Drielandenpunt, which translates to Three Lands Point. At the edge of the small Dutch town of Vaals marks the meeting of The Netherlands, Germany and Belgium. It is said that over one million visitors go there every year.

Andrea wrote an endearing poem for this special town of Vaals and presented it to the city's Mayor Van Leent. Left of Andrea, in the photo below, is John Brauers, at the time Director of the VVV (the Vaals Tourist Information Center). Andrea is presenting a plaque which incorporated the special landmark in his lovely design.

An Ode to Vaals

From Vaals, we look at many lands
And grasp with greetings friendly hands,
Germany-Belgium-Netherlands all,
Here, within a boundary fall.

On peaceful borders people live
A meaning to life they cheerfully give
The world with pride does proudly say,
Visit Vaals, spend a happy day.

Upon hearing the news by the European Commission that they were to begin the opening of borders, Andrea, in Vaals at the time, began writing a poem which shows his excitement of the event to come.

Free Europe

Borders fade in '93
Europe now may be quite free

Commerce sure can have its day
Life will know a better way

A hope for the future, The World to see
United Europe '93

Denmark

On a visit to Copenhagen, Denmark, Andrea saw the famous statue of the Little Mermaid and was inspired by her certain "poetic license". She symbolizes the adventure by Danish poet, Hans Christian Anderson, which tells of a mermaid who fell in love with a prince from land. She agrees to give up her tongue in exchange for legs that could only take painful steps. As a poet, Andrea recognized her significance and spoke to her with a poem:

Little Mermaid

Little mermaid on the rock
The ocean is your only frock
As you look out to the sea
What wonders there they be.

Neptune guards you Heaven sent
With his reigning trident
Daughter of the mighty blue
In ecstasy I look at you.

Spain

When Andrea first visited Spain at the young age of 12, he fell in love for the first time. When he came to Spain as a grown man, he fell in love again when he first set eyes on his wife, Catherine.

They became completely enchanted with the wonderful coastal town of Torremolinos, located on the "Costa del Sol" near Malaga and would live there four or five months out of each year. Inspired by its coastal waters and beauty, Andrea said he "heard music in the streets" and felt free to sing as he strolled the town on those enchanted evenings. He was a visiting professor at the University of Malaga, teaching journalism, English and American History.

Andrea wrote many poems of love for his second home. Here are only a few:

Spanish and Sunrise

The sun shines on the mountains and it rises from the sea
On the beaches hard at work the fishermen there be

Pulling in the nets by hand singing as they go
While tourists line the beaches as if to see a show.

Children play upon the sands while lovers stroll and sing
Far off in the distance the chapel bells ring

'Tis Spain for sure I know it well, and were it all a dream,
I'd dream it every time I could, for I love so well the theme.

Seen here with his students, the topic of his
class that day was the Egyptian Pyramids.

Malaga

In Malaga, there is a song I hear
A melody from a distant sphere

Light and lilting, lovely and sweet
You can hear it play on any street

The harbor great havens busy ships
There in port from ocean trips

Seamen stroll from ships to bars
Fountains smile 'neath twinkling stars

Church bells chime the hours away
Malaga, where my soul does stay.

Torremolinos

Where fair winds kiss a tranquil sea,
And clouds seem to play a symphony.

Where lovers walk by beaches bright,
Kiss by the moon's enchanting light.

All the world stands blissfully still,
Call it Torremolinos, if you will.

When The Poet and his wife were traveling from Spain to Holland, they passed by Salamanca, in northern Spain. Somewhere in back of a house, Andrea discovered a Model A Ford. He was struck by the moment and wrote this delightful poem for the poor vehicle:

On the Road to Salamanca

On the road to Salamanca
We found a Model A,
And when I asked the man the price
It was much to my dismay.

"One thousand dollars, cash", he said
And never blinked an eye.
That price for such a car,
The thing should really fly!

The tires were flat, and the wheels were square,
The glass had gone to rest,
The inside of the body
Looked exactly like a pest.

How on earth could anyone
Ask or pay that price
He looked, I looked, and the people there
Were forced to look just twice.

Two fools, they said, had really met
And it was plain to see
The story that I am pleased to tell,
Is of a Model A and me

A Tree

(poem written for the first Convention in Torremolinos, Spain)

I asked of a tree
What it planned to be
What future it desired

The tree said to me
If a poem I could be
Then man would be truly inspired

Time went along
And the woods sang a song
The trees were all turned to paper

A poet came by
With his eyes in the sky
And extracted that wish from the vapor

The tree is a book
Filled with beautiful verse
This though you may always remember

A tree in the woods
A book on the shelf
Do themselves, hold this origin of splendor

Mingling with classmates of King Juan Carlos of Spain.

Gibraltar

Andrea visited Gibraltar several times and was influenced by its seas, the "rock" and its amazing lighthouses. He often went to Europe on business and cultural missions, in the hopes of promoting good relations with the European business world. His goal was to bring business to the United States and the Philadelphia area, in particular at the Navy Shipyard.

Gibraltar

Straits of Gibraltar
Gateway to Cathay
Sail East or West
You will arrive there one day.

Eastward through Suez
Westward across the Isthmus
Sailing West
Touching the Isles of Christmas

Sail around the world
And surely you will see
The Madonna of Europe
Rich in history.

Kowloon to Gibraltar

From Kowloon to Gibraltar
Is a long, long way
Through Suez or Panama
You can go either way

With a seabag of poems
And a song in your heart
Makes no difference
From whence you start

Lighthouses big
Or lighthouses small
Sail and sail
You will see them all

Remember this story
And keep it in mind
When you sail to heaven
Lighthouses you will find.

On a visit to Gibraltar in 1989, Andrea cruised the sea on the M.V. Coronia. Here, in his own words, is an article he wrote of this experience and the poem that resulted from it:

"No trip to Gibraltar would ever be complete without a harbor cruise on the M.V. Coronia. The ship sails from Gibraltar Harbor out into the straits where one can get a fantastic view of the "Rock". The Coronia, skippered by Michael Zammitt, is a ship that speaks for herself; a magnificent recorded tape plays as you cruise and tells a history of the gallant Coronia that saved so many lives in the Battle of Dunkirk. In fact she flies at her bow the flag of St. George, decorated with the Coat of Arms of Dunkirk for her gallantry. For all tourists visiting Gibraltar a cruise on the Coronia is well worth their while."

Andrea was so inspired that he wrote this poem in the wheelhouse of that famous ship:

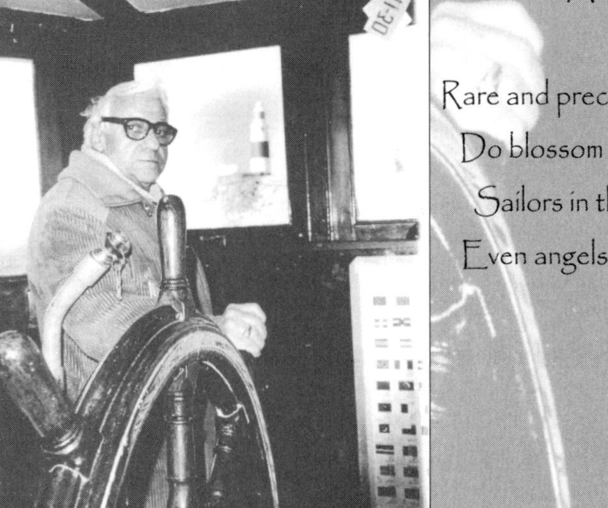

M.V. Coronia

From Dunkirk to Gibraltar
In harbor now she lies
Coronia, ship of valor
'Neath the sunny skies

Extolling the Rock's Great History
Her voyage with stories true
Bringing the straits and harbor lights
All in scenic view

Rare and precious moments
Do blossom from this ship
Sailors in the harbor say
Even angels make the trip

Egypt

In Egypt, Andrea was moved to write poems for this amazing "Wonder of the World":

Pyramids

Did we not build the pyramids You and I
That adorn the sunset sky

That speak to man and do knowledge impart
Of science and works of art

All this was done in yesteryears
May the words we speak please the angels' ears

POET PYRAMID

A poet lived in a pyramid
A pyramid of gold
From its magic doorway
Stories did unfold
Just where they came from
Was baffling to the mind
They came from another sphere
That only poets find

Italy

Andrea's visit to Rome brought him to the famous Trevi Fountain, arguably the most beautiful fountain in Rome. Here the dashing and debonair Poet is tossing coins in the fountain for good luck, while in the setting, the fountain's central figure of Neptune, God of the Sea, rides his chariot of seahorses.

Neptune

Neptune's treasures of the sea
Are hidden by the century.

Safe from wars, battles, and plight
They rest 'neath the waves in a hidden night.

What pirate or storm or a wreck far at sea,
Sent treasures so rare, where so safe they would be.

Now into today man ventures below
One by one, Neptune's treasures here do show.

The gift to mankind, from ages gone by,
Neptune's bounty so great, a feast to the eye

In Italy, Andrea went on a visit to Napoli. He was so struck by their driving habits, he wrote this sweet and comical poem:

Napoli 1987

Every car is bent or broken
This is just a little token

Of how they drive in Napoli
Drive as if they're on a spree

Horns that blow, brakes that squeal
Give the gas and hold the wheel

Give her the gun and off we go
One more dent will never show

Greece

Andrea's visit to Greece certainly piqued his poetic creativity. The Acropolis and its history, the picturesque islands and the surrounding sea, brought words easily from head to paper. Andrea felt such inspiration with Greece's history, culture and the beauty of her islands, he captures his enthusiasm in these next poems:

The Owl

An owl of Athena,
Did converse with me
He sat on a stone,
And not in a tree

He looked at the stars,
As they shone in the night
He sang songs of old,
And hooted with delight.

A stranger I was,
But was treated with care
As we sat on a hill,
And enjoyed the night air

Athens did sleep,
As the world went its way
The owl talked to me,
Till the dawn of the day.

Acropolis

Athens speaks through the sands of time
Acropolis, a work divine

Centuries bid you as they pass
Endowing culture on every class

Athena, Goddess of wisdom rare
Did with an owl indulge her care

And set forth for all the world to see
The Parthenon, rich in history

A. Lippi

Captain Lippi was so fond of Greece's marine life that the only captain's hat he dared to wear was an authentic Greek sailor's hat. He was given sailor hats from all over the world throughout his life, but after his first visit to Greece in the 1950's, he wore only the Greek one.

Santorini

What harbor glows in sun so bright
And twinkles like the stars at night
Welcomes mermaids as they pass
Waters clear as crystal glass

Rising from the sea of light
With all your splendor dressed in white
You are like a dream I know so well
Ancient mariners your stories tell

Oh Santorini, will I return?
Knowing that for you I yearn
Here to spend a treasured day
Isle of beauty, for you I pray

Hydra

Hydra, a port in the Aegean Sea
Is all a harbor e'er should be
Shops and bars, with colors so rare
Lend beauty to boats, as they call there

Workboats and yachts, ka-iki's and gigs
Lend color to all, with their nautical rigs
What more to desire on the rim of the sea
This small Grecian port looks like heaven to me.

Israel

When Andrea visited Israel, he felt such spirituality in the air, he wrote his feelings in a poem, which he presented to the Prime Minister of Israel, David Ben-Gurion. The poem found a permanent home in the opera house in Tel Aviv.

Israel

Israel, Israel how I love thee!
Heaven has blessed the skies above thee

In thy temple prayers ascending
True, thy faith is never ending

Heaven hear me, that I pray
Oh Lord, bless Israel today

Rosh Hashanah
A Poem for the Jewish New Year

While the New Year's candles burn and glow,
Let the Holy wine freely flow.
For New Year is here with joy and cheer,
Thoughts of love for one so dear.

Summer's work is at an end,
Bountiful gift does the good earth send.
To the children of God who worship tonight,
May they always walk in the Holy Light.

Mediterranean Mosaic

Mediterranean Mosaic
Cast by the sands of time
From the Atlantic to the Red Sea
You are a frame of mind

Morocco with its Casbah
Spain with its Sunny Coast
Italy, wine and music
Art you cherish most

France at the Riviera
Egypt your River Nile
Mediterranean Mosaic
Where man does spend a while

Hawaii

Andrea was so intrigued with Hawaii, that through the years he visited what he thought to be "one of the most magnificent vacation places". When Hawaii became the 50th State in August of 1959, Andrea had to be there, doing what he did best. He did television and radio presentations for the new state throughout the United States and Europe, co-sponsored by the Hawaii Visitor's Bureau and United States Overseas Airlines. Andrea was director of public relations for the airline at that time and was accredited with being one of the prime movers in the development and promotion of Hawaii as a tourist mecca.

This next picture is of Andrea presenting his poem, which he had engraved on a plaque, to the then Governor, William Quinn, in 1960, commemorating the Achievement of Statehood for the islands.

AN ODE TO HAWAII

HAWAII, ISLE OF JOY AND PLEASURE
BEAUTY THERE TOO GREAT TO MEASURE

HIGHLANDS REACHING TO THE SKY
BEACHES WHERE THE SEA BIRDS FLY

MUSIC FILLS YOUR EVERY DAY
CROWNED WITH A FLOWER SCENTED LEI

PARADISE PACIFIC ISLE
GOD HAS BLESSED YOU WITH A SMILE

ALOHA WEEK

In nautical flight
From Molokai to Waikiki
Indeed a wonderful
Sight to see

O'er the tropic blue
They streak
For this is the start
Of ALOHA WEEK

Hawaii
Beach boys play upon the sands
Famous in Hawaiian lands
Neptune's sons they surf the wave
Joy and song their beings crave
Palm trees sway - the breezes sing
Hawaii, oh what joys you bring

Robert Louis Stevenson, Mark Twain and Andrea Lippi had many things in common. One was that they were all inspired by the Banyan Trees on Waikiki Beach. Banyan trees grow to enormous size by sending down aerial roots that can grow more than half a foot each month to stabilize the trunk. These trees produced poems, stories and songs about Hawaii.

Andrea presented his poem, "The Banyan Tree" to the manager of the Moana Hotel.

The Banyan Tree

I stood on the beach in Waikiki
Under a Banyan Tree
The starry night and the rolling waves
Sent a stillness over me

Torches burned, and the natives sang
What could the answer be?
Paradise before my eyes
On the beach at Waikiki

Panama Canal

Andrea wrote a poem for the Panama Canal and had it published in many local papers. He loved telling stories, especially to children, and tried to inspire them with simple poetic history by sometimes printing articles just for them.

Andrea's own drawing

An Ode To The Panama Canal

Steamers waiting for the locks
Some in harbor some in docks

One by one, two by two
In their turn they follow through

Locks are steps that steamers climb
Saving ships both work and time

A vital link in all world trade
The great huge locks by man were made.

Florida

Everyone loves Florida, and Andrea was no exception. Her sunny skies and glorious beaches could only result in poems. Here are only a couple:

An Ode to Florida

Lord, when you made Florida,
You made the sun to shine.
You made the palm trees whisper,
In a land of honey and wine.

You made the ocean beaches
And lakes where Flamingos fly.
Lord, when you made Florida,
'Twas the apple of Heaven's eye.

My Home Is The Miami River

My home is the Miami River
From Biscayne to the Glades,
Winding weaving River
Void of palisades.

But kissed and loved by palm trees,
Blessed by sunny skies,
Ships sail from your harbors
Right before our eyes.

To islands in the oceans
Ports throughout the world,
A weaving tropic river
Your beauty is unfurled.

A. Lippi

Andrea wrote the next poem in Miami when visiting Marineland. He presented it to AUTEC - Atlantic Undersea Test and Evaluation Center in West Palm Beach and it was published in their employee publication:

The depths of the seas hold mysteries
Far beyond compare,
A look at the rise of Neptune's skies
Behold what magic there.

Dolphins that speak in a native tongue
Turtles that float on a cloud,
Darting fish with colors bright
Mammals that cry aloud.

The Ocean's floor resembles the land
With mountain valleys and plains,
When man does enter Neptune's realm
What beauty he proclaims.

Talk about fabulous pictures! It didn't get much better than this for the romantic poet, as we can clearly see on his face. He is seen here with his lovely wife and their new friends.

At Marineland in Florida, Andrea makes friends with a whale named Kay.

I Met A Whale

I met a whale
Beside a beach,
I was astounded
By his speech.

His grammar was
Of such delight
His eyes did flash,
With a sparkling light.

"Good Friend," he said,
"I have come to hear
The poems you have written
In many a year!"

Without delay I did recite
The poems you will hear
This very night.

While visiting the Speed Weeks program at Daytona Beach in March of 1957, Andrea wrote the official poem for the race that year:

(Daytona Beach poem)
"Speed Weeks" Put To Verse

The Angels have gotten the beaches ready
The crowds on the dunes and in the stands.
The drivers warm up their trusty cars
The wheel in their steady hands.

A PRAYER in their heart for victory
Hoping for success.
Some will realize their fondest dreams
Others will settle for less.

They're off and the race has started
'Round and 'round they go,
Into the pits and out again,
The tide is still quite low.

The finish will crown the victor
To fame and glory he'll leap,
The race is won for another year –
What speeds will the future reap?

The Poet is seen here with his Dodge Wayfarer convertible coupe with a 6 cyl. engine, driven - at the time - an impressive 100 mph on the racing sands.

Bahamas

Eastward of Miami
Are islands to be sure
The Bahamas rich with beauty
Filled with tropic lure

Beach hats wide and sunny
Water crystal clear
Just a line to let you know
We wish that you were here

Canada

To mark Canada's 110th birthday on July 1st 1977, Andrea wrote a special poem for the good neighbor of the United States and presented it to the citizens for their annual celebration:

Canada's Birthday, 1977

From the Atlantic to the Pacific
From the States to the Arctic Sea
There is friendly Canada
Nation just and free

Her mountains and her prairies
Her rocky rugged shore
Lakes that shine beneath the stars
For angels to explore

One of Andrea's biggest honors was his invitation to Halifax, Nova Scotia for their tribute to the Battle of the Atlantic and the more than 100 corvettes (navy ships) and the men who sailed aboard them.

Andrea had written a poem for the Canadian Navy after he saw a vision, from the "depths of his being" of "a mountainous wave break over the bow of a corvette as it plowed through the treacherous waters of the Atlantic". He immediately began to recite a poetic tribute to these ships. The Canadian Corvettes provided coastal escort and mine clearing work for the Canadian Navy from 1939 to 1945. They were also ocean escorts for naval warships and merchant ships that crossed the Atlantic for British Duty. This was difficult and dangerous and held high casualties.

Andrea contacted Canadian officials and told them of his poem. Canada's Minister of National Defense, at the time, Arthur C. Eggleton, responded to Andrea's letter and invited him to present his poem on May 6, 2000 during their commemorative ceremonies in Halifax. The poet in return was presented with a plaque to show their gratitude for his dedication to the Corvettes.

Andrea with Rear Admiral D.E. Miller.

And so it was - this most special honor of presenting his poems, what he loved to do the most - would be his last hurrah and his last trip on this earth.

Courageous Canadian Corvettes

Corvettes battled
The Winter Sea
On their course
To victory

Mountainous waves
Winds like a knife
All lead
To hell and strife

But dauntless they were
Dauntless they be
Sailing o'er
The heavenly sea
A famous chapter
In Canadian history

Dauntless Corvettes

Guardian angels were they
Through the night
And through the day
Escorting the convoys on their way

Wolf packs stalked
Their very course
Reporting positions
On the morse

Devastation and death
Woven into every hour
Their faith in the Almighty
Was their greatest power

Of the dauntless corvettes
Are the stories told
Their valor at sea
Does forever unfold

Andrea made an adventure out of every place he visited and felt traveling exposed the mind and opened the heart. Throughout his life, The Poet met thousands of people all over the world, and wherever he went, he was welcomed with open arms. All who met him were undoubtedly left with fond memories and a first-rate impression of an American poet with a great enthusiasm for living - always on a pursuit for inspiration.

Andrea was a true "Patriot" in every sense of the word and felt an extraordinary commitment to his country. "Expressions of patriotism are what keep us together as a people", he would say. And Andrea went beyond the norm to fulfill a duty he felt was a "calling".

Andrea did everything for the love of his country, her people, and her defenders. Perhaps the Hon. William J. Hughes of New Jersey said it best when he approached the House of Representatives on Thursday, August 28, 1980:

"Mr. Speaker, the word 'patriotism' too long out of vogue, is enjoying a much needed renaissance in our country. Recently, one of my constituents, Dr. Andrea Lippi of Somers Point, NJ, gave me a copy of his poem, "Say Something Good About America." The thought expressed by Dr. Lippi's verse are good advice for all of us. Now is the time to reflect upon the good things in our country that we all take for granted. The text of Dr. Lippi's poem follows," This was published in the Congressional Record of that day:

Say Something Good About America

Say something good about America,
Praise her every day.
Say something good about America,
For 'tis here we work and pray.

Say something good about America,
The land we love so true.
Say something good about America,
America, I love you.

Andrea loved America and all the diverse beauty she possesses. Throughout his travels around the globe, he spoke of her with love and adoration, and carried poems about America wherever he went:

Visit America, U.S.A.

Visit America, U.S.A.
A wonderful place to travel and play

Beautiful country from coast to coast
Things to see, you will enjoy the most

Cities with buildings up to the sky
Beaches where seabirds glide and fly

Prairies where cowboys tend their herds
Grand Canyon, the Rockies; too marvelous for words

Florida, Texas, California and the south
The great Mississippi, New Orleans, the mouth

Seattle, Wisconsin, Great Falls and the lakes
Chicago, Detroit, Niagara; it breaks

See this great country, the east and the west
VISIT AMERICA – "the place" you'll like best.

The simplicity of some of Andrea's writings is meant to get children excited about the nation as well as her history.

Faith and a dream is all that we need,
To carry us on like a galloping steed.

With eyes to the future let us pray,
God Bless America and the American Way

God Bless our Nation

God bless our nation while we sleep,
And angels all a vigil keep.
Guard our shores and borderlands.
Our destiny is in Your hands.

Amen

After the "Address to the Nation" in 1989 in which the President spoke of his concern about the drug problem in America, Andrea immediately wrote a special prayer and mailed it to the White House with a letter to the President that same night. Andrea introduced himself as a "patriotic American", and felt it was his duty to help the situation in any way he could.

Our Nation Free from Drugs

Almighty God
To Thee we pray
Free our land
From drugs today

Save our nation
From this horrible curse
The caverns of hell
Or even worse

With this fervent prayer
We ask of Thee
May our nation and the world
From drugs be free

Andrea was devoted to the "war on drugs" and also wrote this next poem, which he presented to Commissioner Robert Armstrong.

Lies are bad drugs are worse
Lies and drugs are children's curse.

So don't tell lies from drugs stay away
Your life can be a happy day

The Patron Saint of Policemen

Saint Michael,
Strong and true
Adversary of Satan
We rely on you.

Keep us safe and healthy
Our families free from harm
May we walk through earth and heaven
With this prayer as our sacred charm

Andrea was asked to write a poem for a Police Memorial Service that was held in January of 1989, and he joyfully came through. With Andrea's intervention, the same poem was also read in Spain on the same day in St. Michael's Church and was read by Fr. Francisco Apericio before a congregation of over 850 people. This was to celebrate police officers all over the world. The mass in Spain was recorded and sent to radio stations in the U.S.

Patriotism is the magnet which drew Andrea to truly celebrate Independence Day. Andrea's special message on that day: "All it takes is a little kindness. You don't need armies, navies or guns….just kindness".

On the 4th of July, Andrea would put on his colonial suit and enjoy this most important day. One was sure to find him among a crowd of people, reciting his poetry and charming his listeners with a patriotic message.

Independence Day

Celebrate our freedom
Keep America free,
That is a task for us all to do
On land and on the sea

Steeped Proud in tradition
Our flag waves in the sky
Honored to say God Bless this Day
This memorable Fourth of July

A Poet's Pledge of Allegiance

The Liberty Bell rang out on the Port that day
Alerting ships that in harbor lay

Freedom had come to the very land
All had happened as Heaven planned

A flag would fly over land and sea
Indeed a banner of Liberty

Andrea at the Liberty Bell as a young boy.

Until the end of his days, Andrea remembered vividly when he was a 23-year old young man, and he heard the news that Pearl Harbor had been attacked. Through the years, he always remembered the tragedy of that day and the over 2,000 men who lost their lives.

In November of 1956, Andrea saw a television special about the attack on Pearl Harbor, which prompted him to write a poem. He then flew to Honolulu to be at the 15th Anniversary ceremonies on December 7th. He placed a wreath on the resting place of the USS Arizona, the site of the Pearl Harbor Memorial. He participated in the ceremony by reading his poem, which was dedicated to the military personnel who died on that day.

He also took with him 1000 copies of the poem, which he printed on postcards, and had them postmarked "Pearl Harbor, Dec. 7". He then sent them back to the States, mailing the first postcard to President Dwight Eisenhower. The poem reads:

Pearl Harbor Anniversary Poem

We will remember December 7
Day of Infamy
When planes flew in and bombed our fleet
And murdered the sons of the free

It threw our nation into war
Thank God, we won the fight
The lesson learned at Pearl Harbor
Must never fade from our sight

Pearl Harbor

The day they bombed Pearl Harbor
Is the day they bombed Berlin
That is the day that Hitler's grasp
Began to wear quite thin

USA and the allies
All got in the fight
The meaning of Democracy
Showed its strength and might

The crewmen of the Arizona
Live in history's hourglass
The bell rings out for freedom
As time does graciously pass

This first trip to Pearl Harbor began a tradition for Andrea. He continued to write poetry honoring that tragic day and, as often as he could, attended anniversary ceremonies in Hawaii on December 7th. He always placed a wreath at the memorial, which he brought all the way from Cape May, made of holly and native pine. He would recite his heartfelt poems dedicated to the remembrance of "The Day of Infamy".

Andrea seen here with the Rear Admiral William H. Leahy, Shipyard Commander.

In December of 1959, Andrea again took the trip to Pearl Harbor and took with him a wreath, which was blessed by the Rev. Dr. John Craig Roak, Rector of the Old Swedes Church in Independence Hall, Philadelphia. After the blessing, the wreath was turned over to Andrea, to timely take with him on his flight to Hawaii, to place at the USS Arizona during anniversary ceremonies.

Also attending services that year at Pearl Harbor was Rear Admiral A.A. Solomons, commandant of the 14th Naval District. In this next photo, Andrea stands proudly next to the Admiral.

Andrea had quite a passion for the USS Arizona for it held major significance in Pearl Harbor. On December 7, 1941 at around 8:00 am, a Japanese Zero's bomb hit the ship, exploding and sinking the vessel. The crew of 1,177 perished, and most remain entombed in the Arizona's rusted hull. In US Naval history, no other ship has taken so many down with her. Many ships were sunk on December 7th, but the Arizona represents all who died that day. The Arizona Memorial is visited annually by 1.5 million people.

In 1960, Andrea was not able to attend the ceremonies in Hawaii but that did not stop him. His commemorative poem was read by remote telephone hookup. The call was placed from the Information Bureau office at the Wildwood boardwalk and was broadcast over Hawaiian radio networks at the time of the ceremonies on the deck of the Arizona.

A PSALM FOR PEARL HARBOR

Heroes of Pearl Harbor
Their bodies lie in state
For their souls entered heaven
Passed through the Pearly Gate

The 7th of December
Goes down in history
A treacherous act....
A day of Infamy

When unable to go to Pearl Harbor, Andrea would attend ceremonies every December 7th at the Liberty Bell, always with a wreath and a poem. In 1991, the 50th Anniversary of Pearl Harbor, Andrea, at the Liberty Bell, found himself with the now *former* Rear Admiral A.A. Solomons. Thirty-two years later, both found themselves together again, devoted to the remembrance and commemoration of Pearl Harbor and the Arizona.

That year, Andrea gave a dramatic reading of his poem titled USS Arizona Memorial:

USS Arizona Memorial

Arizona. Be it ever remembered
Let men just speak her name.
She has joined the fleets immortal
On the seas of undying fame.

Her memory survives as always
A part of our nation's pride.
Men will live to praise the sailors
Who struggled there and died.

There are no troubled waters
For these men now lie in state.
God chose them to be his crewmen
And sent them to heaven to wait.

Gabriel knows their number
And he calls them all by name,
When crewmen up in heaven
Share Arizona's fame.

"Amens" went up from the crowd after the last line was read.

In the year 1990, the United Nations took action to liberate Kuwait from occupying Iraqi forces. During Operations Desert Shield and Desert Storm, Andrea was in full support of the U.S. troops and the cause that took them to the Persian Gulf. Andrea once again put pen to paper:

From Jersey Shore
To Desert Shield
A prayer we say;
Keep our troops
Free from harm
Help them
In every way.

God find a way
To keep the peace
Let understanding reign
If war does come
And battles rage
May victory
We proclaim.

Only hours after Desert Shield started, the preliminary preparations for Desert Storm, Andrea showed his patriotism and support of the troops by planting a cross on the Cape May beach. A strong believer in the Majesty of God, he wanted to create a type of shrine that was open for all to go and pray for the safe return of the soldiers serving in the Persian Gulf. "People can now come here and pray for their boys and everyone overseas. It is a free place to pray. This is God's land," said Andrea.

**Andrea, helped by two friends, Dan Marino &
David Wand, a US Navy medic who served in
Korea and Vietnam.**

But this was not enough for Andrea and he felt the need to do more. Andrea made two replicas of the Cape May Beach monument and sent them to President Bush and General Schwartzkopf together with his poems. The small crosses were made from cuttings of the original.

Andrea making crosses.

A. Lippi

A Salute to General Schwarzkopf

Desert Storm is over
Old Glory waves on high
Yellow ribbons grace the land
Pleasing to the eye.

Schwartzkopf won the battle
The President did so too.
Everything here on in
Is up to me and you

Our nation is built on justice
With liberty for all
Prayers of thanks to almighty God
Must be our every call.

SALUTING THE 253rd

From the Jersey Shore to the Jersey Shore
Many moons have passed.
Memories of the Middle East
Forever more will last

Yellow ribbons claim the day
Cheers and kisses too
Our beloved America
We fought and won for you.

COMMANDER IN CHIEF
UNITED STATES CENTRAL COMMAND
MACDILL AIR FORCE BASE, FLORIDA 33608-7001

12 June 1991

Dear Andrea Lippi,

I want to express my sincere thanks for your letter voicing support for me and our valiant troops. Also, thank you for the poems. The tremendous outpouring of encouragement by the American people has been the foundation and driving force behind our success in both Operation Desert Shield and Operation Desert Storm.

You and thousands like you have provided us the strength and determination to liberate Kuwait and fulfill the United Nations Resolutions. It is because of this visible demonstration of concern for our soldiers, sailors, airmen, marines and coastguardsmen that we in the military are proud to be serving our country and its citizens.

Again, thank you as we look forward to the day when our last service member returns to the shores of our great nation.

Sincerely,

H. NORMAN SCHWARZKOPF
General, U.S. Army

Andrea received a beautiful letter of gratitude from
Gen. Schwarzkopf of which he was most proud.

A poem written during the Vietnam War:

Vietnam

We have added our stars to the heavens above
As old glory flies on through the night
Remembering those in far Vietnam,
Who for Liberty and Freedom do fight

Their valor and strife their sacrifice great.
Is a part of our nation's pride
With a prayer in our heart and reverence profound
May the angels be at their side.

Throughout his life, Andrea was a man dedicated to his country, her armed forces, as well as the future of her children. He did what he could in support, using his God-given talents for the good, always on a mission of patriotic poetry.

They Will Not Have Died In Vain

They Will Not Have Died In Vain
If we are ready to fight again

If we fail to rally for the cause that's just
We will then have betrayed our sacred trust

Uphold our Constitution!

ndrea's interests were vast and reached from the heavens, in both a physical and spiritual sense, to the bottom of the sea. Once he was excited about something, there was no stopping him.

When Astronauts Neil Armstrong, Michael Collins and Edwin Aldrin embarked on their mission to the moon, Andrea had to be at the scene. On July 16, 1969 at Cape Kennedy, Florida, Andrea eagerly waited the launch.

He stood with Apollo 11 just before takeoff, and wished it well with a poem he wrote for the occasion:

Ode to Apollo II

The heavens open to welcome man
Human from earth with a flag in his hand.

Old Glory will fly from the moon with great pride,
Man's future in space will be taken in stride.

Thank God for our wisdom, bless our Astronauts three
Men from America, land of the free.

Futurevision

The Heavens and skies do miracles hold
Who can tell what the future enfolds.
A base on the moon, a man on Mars-
Needless to say, we'll conquer the stars

Great Mother Earth, the universe beckons.
Horizons new open in seconds
God in His wisdom his infinite plan
Has opened the Heavens to Earth's mortal man.

Andrea always felt charged when it came to his faith and spirituality. It is shown in the majority of his poems, glorifying God, praying for the Divine to watch over us, and writing of the "heavens" with excitement and praise.

I Saw an Angel

I saw an Angel kneeling
Underneath a tree
He never said a single word
And yet he spoke to me

For those who pray there is heaven
For those with faith it's true
No matter 'neath what tree you pray
The angel prays with you.

Heaven – A Wonderful Place

Heaven is such a wonderful place
No difference there in color or race

All are equal – religion and Creed
Faith in God is all you need

Prayers and blessings are all the same
Return to Heaven from whence you came

All Men

They say all men have work to do
If to themselves, they will be true
To make the world a better place
A haven for the human race

Serve their God and be a friend
To the needy their help they send
Those who work with hearts so true
Help God build the world anew.

Andrea's fascination of the Sea as a young boy carried over to his years as an adult. When he began writing poetry, he favored topics of the sea and marine life. In 1953 he had enough poems to publish a book called "Sea of Faith". Andrea considered himself an oceanographer and an eminent authority on matters of the sea. He took great pride in this book and carried several copies with him on his travels around the globe. He had the books stamped at customs as proof that his books traveled around the world.

In the picture below, taken in 1956, Andrea is presenting copies of his book to visiting delegates from Spain, Holland and Surinam at the 45th Annual Convention of the American Association of Port Authorities in Philadelphia:

My Dream of Ships
I dream of ships that come and go;
Ships that sail where trade winds blow.
Ships that hail from a foreign port;
Ships with cargo of every sort.

Freighters fast and freighters slow;
Famous ships with names we know.
The dreams that I dream are of ships and the sea.
Won't you share a dream with me?

Blue Lagoons

Give me the blue lagoons
Where the cockatoo croons

Where the mocking bird wings
Where the nightingale sings

There in the islands I long to stay
Where the beaches are white where the flying fish play

Under the palms by the rim of the sea
My tropical isle is heaven to me

Retired Seaman

The wind can blow and the tide can raise
But safe in their pasture my cattle will graze.
For I've left the sea this autumn day,
And dry ashore I intend to stay.

Gone are my days before the mast,
The wintry seas and Neptune's blast.
Torrid nights by a tropic shore
With shipmates crying, "Never more!"

Dry on a farm I'll settle down
And ride my buckboard into town;
Stop at the store and get my mail
Follow the deer and the possum's trail.

A sailor I was, but a farmer I'll be;
The sea has seen the last of me.

In 1967, Andrea was asked to write a poem on the sea for the Oceanographic Consortium in Miami, FL. At that meeting, Andrea met and befriended a man named Scott Carpenter. Mr. Carpenter had a dual title of Astronaut/Aquanaut. He served as backup pilot for John Glenn during the first manned orbital flight and flew the second American orbital flight in May of 1962. Carpenter also participated in the Navy's Man-in-the-Sea project and was Director of Aquanaut Operations for the Navy's Deep Submergence Systems Project (DSSP). Upon retirement from the Navy in 1969, Carpenter founded and became CEO of Sear Sciences, Inc., a corporation developing programs aimed at the enhancement and utilization of ocean resources and improved health of the planet.

Andrea was quite proud to know this man of such importance and who had so much in common with him. He shared the story many times of their acquaintance and of Scott Carpenter's tributes to the study of our planet.

Presenting a poem to Scott Carpenter at the Oceanographic Consortium in Miami.

In the picture above, Andrea is seen standing proudly with the very tall and very famous Jacques Piccard, a deep-sea explorer, inventor and marine designer from Switzerland. Piccard and his father, Auguste, built the *Trieste,* a bathyscaphe or self-propelled deep-sea ship used to travel the ocean floor. The deepest undersea voyage up to that point was in January of 1960 by Jacques Piccard and Don Walsh of the US Navy in the *Trieste.* Piccard's inventions only escalated from there; perfecting vessels for greater depth and maneuverability.

Piccard was bestowed such honors as the Distinguished Public Service Award by Dwight D. Eisenhower; the Science and Engineering Award of the Drexel Institute; the Theodore Roosevelt Distinguished Service medal; honorary memberships in the Swiss Institute of Naval Architects and the National Geographic Society; as well as others too numerous to mention.

Andrea had a deep admiration for Jacques Piccard as well as Scott Carpenter. He carried these pictures of them in his wallet, to proudly show and tell of their meeting and the oceanographic contributions of these two men.

Many people are fascinated with the tragic story of the Titanic and Andrea was no exception. He researched it extensively, going as far as creating sketches of his own interpretation of the tragic scene. He found generic pictures of sailing vessels and painted and blotted white paint in the background, creating the massive iceberg that brought down the ship.

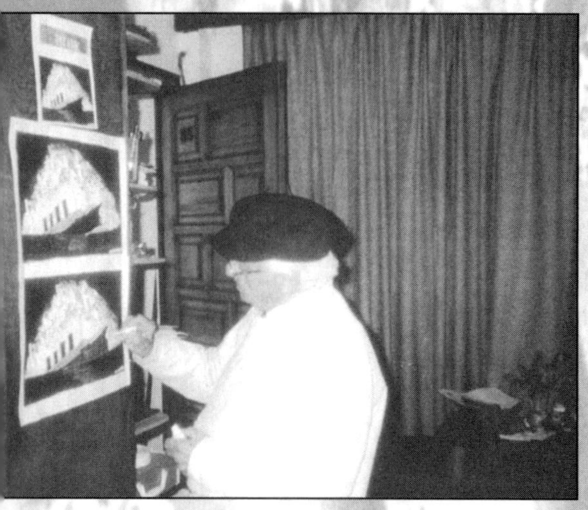

Andrea learned things about the Titanic that were little known to others. He wrote many poems about the vessel and also wrote a series of 17 poems, which tells the entire story of the Titanic from beginning to end in poetic verse. In this book, we will feature only a few:

Tragedy of the Titanic

The night was clear
The ship was fast
Her good fortune
Was not to last

An iceberg loomed
In yonder sea
Causing untold
Tragedy

A lookout shouted
But too late
With disaster
The liner had a date

The Morse was garbled
Did not get through
Help came too late
But to a few

The unsinkable vanished
In an icy sea
Now a part
Of our history

Fascination Beneath the Sea

Titanic lies in yonder realm
Far beneath the sea
Where whales and creatures of every kind
Enjoy life blissfully

Man returned to the sleeping ship
That holds secrets beyond compare
Fascination now haunts the deck
That once knew stark despair.

A. Lippi

In the 1980's, while flying to Spain over the Atlantic Ocean, at the nearest possible location of where the Titanic went down, Andrea recited his poems in tribute to the Titanic, once again, charming the crew and passengers on board.

The Woe of a Gallant Ship

Nearer my God to thee.
Were strains that were heard o'er the icy sea

As the liner made ready to slide away
Ne'er to see the light of day

Panic and fright were part of the night
When tragedy struck with all its might

Took the lives of young and old
That is the way the story was told

There were those who lived to tell the tale
Of a gallant ship that ne'er would sail

Andrea with Captain Michael Spiller of Swiss Air.

Fate or Destiny

Her forward stack did touch the sea,
Within minutes the ship would no more be

But disappeared to the ocean floor
Where she will rest "forever more"

Gallant liner it is sad to say
Courageous fortune came your way

So many perished in an icy sea
Be that fate or destiny

Captive of the Deep

The night was clear the sea was calm
A westward course she lay

Who could ever think
The Titanic would never see the light of day

Scraped into an iceberg with her hull torn apart
Only minutes later, her downward trek did start

Captive of the deep on the ocean floor she lay
With the ingenuity of man, her story comes our way

When Andrea began writing poetry, his subject gravitated towards the sea. He wrote about the beauty of the oceans along with the men and ships that sail the waters and protect her lands. Andrea was surrounded by the sea his entire life and even became the mascot for the Longport, NJ Coast Guard. He shined the brass, cleaned the boats and assisted the men in other duties. He was hooked and subsequently fell in love with the sea. Andrea's first association with submarines was when he and a young friend played in and around the submarines at the Philadelphia Navy Yard.

The Poet's maritime heritage started as a youngster and only advanced in his adulthood. He used his poetry as expressions of gratitude and admiration. That is how he felt about the Navy and the Coast Guard, and he constantly was pulled in their direction.

Andrea was devoted to the sea and thought careers that follow the sea in any way are the "finest possible". He worked extensively with recruiting offices, doing what he did best; advocating Military careers of the sea with poetry and heartfelt words. He had his own Historic Marine Museum in Philadelphia, trying only to raise excitement for careers of the sea. He permitted the children of his neighborhood to use space at his museum as a recreational area. He encouraged them in art, woodworking, and the building of model ships, which he believed was "an excellent means of educating children in a likeness for ships and the sea". In a 1976 interview, he stated, "My beliefs for the times in which we live today, is there is no greater opportunity for our youth than to serve in the US Navy or the Coast Guard. For there, they have security, which is not only financial, but spiritual. They serve their country, they receive an education and they have an opportunity to build a better life for themselves and the people in their community."

He wrote and published many poems about our defending ships; telling of the duties they served. With poems, he honored Navy battleships, and submarines and the crew who served them.

God Bless The Navy

God bless the Navy, the fleets at sea
Sentinels of liberty

Keep them strong in faith and deed
May their hopes and aims succeed

Father, ruler of the sea
With prayers of thanks we worship thee

Victory at Sea

Victory at Sea
Was destined to be
God smiled on the fleets
Of the just and the free.

Salvation with honor
Were heaven's reward
We conquered the man
Who lived by the sword.

In December of 1957, the US Navy Recruiting Station
honored him with a Certificate of Appreciation. It reads:

In Recognition of Outstanding Service
to the
United States Navy
Recruiting Service
this
Certificate of Appreciation
is hereby awarded to

ANDREA LIPPI

INTERNATIONALLY KNOWN POET, AUTHOR AND RETIRED BUSINESSMAN

THROUGH your public-spirited cooperation with the Navy Recruiti[ng] Service, you have contributed immeasurably in furthering the excelle[nt] relations between the United States Navy and the people of your communi[ty.]

In recognition of these services render[ed] so unselfishly, this Certificate [of] Appreciation is presented this 16th d[ay] of December 19 57

W. H. ROGERS JR, Commander, U.S. Nav[y]
Officer in Charge
U.S. Navy Recruiting Station & ONOP[O]
13th & Market Streets
Philadelphia 7, Pennsylvania

178

Andrea's love for submarines lured him to the USS Nautilus, arguably the most famous submarine in the world. She is credited with being the first nuclear submarine, the first submarine to navigate under the North Pole as well as her participation in many endurance exercises that helped to re-write Anti-Submarine Warfare doctrine.

In the picture below taken at the Philadelphia Naval Recruiting Station, Andrea is seen presenting a poem commemorating the polar cruise of the Nautilus to the sub's captain, Cdr. William R. Anderson with Cdr. William H. Rogers, Jr. officer in charge of the Philadelphia Naval Recruiting Station.

Nautilus New Captain and Crew

Captain Nemo could have made the trip
Escaped the Arctic's frozen grip
Anderson in the Nautilus new
Made Jules Verne's dream quite true

On August 3rd, 1958
With destiny the Nautilus had a date
To cross the Pole 'neath a frozen sea
A shining light in history

A well-trained crew did their part
And now the Navy has learned the art
To cross the Pole 'neath a frozen sea
Using atomic energy

In 1958 Andrea was requested by the US Navy to write a poem for the premier of the movie "The Enemy Below". This hit 20th Century Fox film starred Robert Mitchum and Curt Jurgens and was produced and directed by actor Dick Powell.

Andrea composed a poem depicting the non-fiction plot of the movie concerning the dual between a US Destroyer and a German Submarine:

The Enemy Below

Destroyers are fast, courageous and bold
Their course Victory, that's the course that they hold
Dauntless and determined, they fight with a will
Their mission just one to be in on the kill

Our ship was made ready for sonar did know
We were hard on the track of The Enemy Below
To kill or be killed we were in on the show
Our destroyer above the enemy below

A periscope darts through the sea like a knife
This is the start of the hell and the strife
Depth charges, torpedoes exchanged with a will
A brief span of time and the ocean is still

The plans that were made were not made for naught
Our skipper was right, the sub was then caught
A ship died at sea a U-Boat was lost
There are those who will always remember the cost

Tis God whom we thank and grateful we be
The Enemy Below lies lost in the sea

The World Premiere of the motion picture took place at the Fox Theatre in Philadelphia. Andrea recited this poem on the stage of the theatre during special Navy ceremonies before the showing of the film.

Andrea also journeyed to Seattle to present a special award to the officers and men of the Navy ship, USS Whitehurst, for their part in the making of the film. The ship was featured in "The Enemy Below", and was recognized as one of the most accurate stories of destroyers ever filmed. The certificate of excellence was given to Lt. Commander R.K. Prout, Commanding Officer.

The award said: "…an important art vehicle was created which will go far in telling the Navy's story to the people of the United States."

When the famous Italian Navy cruiser, the "Raimondo Montecuccoli", stopped at the Port of Philadelphia in September 1958, Andrea was there to welcome the ship. The Montecuccoli was on a good-will tour carrying midshipmen from the Italian Naval Academy. The vessel has a distinguished history of service in World War II and was honorably discharged to serve in the training of future naval officers. General Montecuccoli, for whom the ship is named, has been a hero for the Italian people for three centuries. The General was born in 1609 and at the age of 16, made the military his career. He participated in a series of battles in the Thirty Years' War and proved himself to be a military genius.

Andrea presented a model of Columbus' ship, the "Santa Maria", to Captain Lamberto del Bene, skipper of the Italian cruiser (left), joined with Commander William H. Rogers, Jr., officer in charge of the US Naval Recruiting Station in Philadelphia.

As the Montecuccoli sailed from the Navy yard back to her homeland, Andrea was overcome with strong feelings and penned the following poem then and there:

Raimondo Montecuccoli
Italian Naval Ship
Arrived in Philadelphia
Here on a good-will trip

The city turned out to greet her
Was great the friends she made
Surely was an inspiring sight
To see the tribute paid

She sailed in early morning
Back to her native land
There were those with a tear in a friendly eye
As they shook a friendly hand

Back home they sing praises
Of a land across the sea
Beautiful America
God's gift to Liberty

Andrea's heartfelt inspiration to write that poem, took him on a mission to Italy less than a month later. He wanted the Captain, the Officers and the Cadets of the Montecuccoli to know the inward and true feelings expressed and generated by their visit. "She won the hearts of Philadelphia people so greatly, I felt that her trip here should be put in a poem for all men to know, for all time, of the great friendship between America and Italy and between their Navies", Andrea stated. He wanted to acknowledge how everyone aboard the Montecuccoli endeared themselves to the people of the US, showing their ship, their uniform and true gracious selves.

The poem first won the admiration of Commander Rogers, Jr., (left) Philadelphia Recruiting Station and Dr. Giovanni Luciolli (right), Italian consul, when Andrea presented them with the finished product. As part of President Eisenhower's "People-to-People" program for improving international friendships, Andrea received their blessing on his upcoming trip to Italy, to present the ode he composed to the officers and men of the Italian ship.

Andrea went to Porto Fario on the Island of Elba, just across the Italian Naval Academy at Livorno and presented his poetic tribute to Admiral Barbera (center} and Captain Lamberto del Bene (right}.

It was received with great enthusiasm, and again, Andrea left the Italian Navy with an honorable impression of America and her gracious people.

In July of 1959, Andrea proudly dedicated a poem at the 169th Anniversary of the founding of the Coast Guard.

The poem was presented to Captain Steinmetz, Commanding Officer of the US Coast Guard at recruit graduation ceremonies at the Cape May Coast Guard Receiving Center.

Angels of the Sea

When there is trouble they call the Coast Guard
No matter where they be
In storm, rain, sleet, and hail
When lost in the angry sea

Adversity has a strong adversary
Thank God so strong they be
When there is trouble they call the Coast Guard
Angels of the Sea

The fifth US Navy vessel of the name USS Triton was named for the Greek merman demigod, son of Poseidon and Amphitrite. USS Triton sailed into history on her maiden voyage when she embarked on Operation Sandblast, the first continuous underwater cruise around the world without surfacing. In February 1960, the Triton left New London, Connecticut and sailed 27,723 miles in 60 days, 21 hours. Under the command of Captain Edward L. "Ned" Beach, the Triton's accomplishment was a clear reaffirmation of US technological supremacy.

When the Atlantic Council of the Navy League visited the submarine in Connecticut, Andrea noted the history-making accomplishment with a poem dedicated to the Triton and crew. Andrea spoke with Captain Beach and presented him with a copy of the poem.

USS Triton
Around the world and under the sea,
Imagine the skill and dexterity!

The Triton did the trick, you know,
Gave the world a wonderful show.

Uncle Sam is proud of his ship
It took the Navy to make the trip!

In 1976, Andrea was one of the press representatives at the "Night In Venice" weekend in Fort Lauderdale, Florida. He presented one of his poems to the Secretary of the Navy, J. William Middendorf.

Write me a Poem

Write me a poem to a poet was said
Cast it in type from hot, smoldering lead

Give it a name as you christen a ship
Put it to sea for its trial maiden trip

Let it float o'er the waves to far away shores
Open men's minds as it opens men's doors

For angels to read as they sit on the stars
May God up above bless the great fleets of ours.

When the USS Coral Sea went to visit the US Navy unit in Naples, Italy, Andrea paid them a visit, as he and his wife were nearby on a visit to the hometown of his ancestors outside of Naples in 1987. He took the opportunity to interview the crew of the ship for his radio/TV programs.

They Fly in Glory

They fly in glory, victory bright
Navy planes, fast and right
Courageous men with wings of gold
Where the swirling battles unfold

Gallant flyers, heroes all,
Born to heed their country's call
So patriotic, tried, and true
America is proud of you

Andrea is seen with Lt. Bob Riviera, Public Relations Officer, learning about the 973-foot carrier.

Flying Coast Guard

Coast Guard copters fly the skies
Search and rescue with magic eyes

Saving souls from perilous seas
Skill and valor of all degrees

Doing the work of God on high
May angels guide them as they fly

In 1989, Andrea helped the US Coast Guard celebrate an occasion of patriotic remembrance with a new poem he presented to Coast Guard Captain, Edward King (right) and Captain Peter Prindle (left):

At the first hint of inspiration, Andrea could remarkably write a poem in a "split second". There is the story of how he wrote the poem "Flagships of Freedom": I was watching TV, one of those morning shows", he recalled, "when I heard British Prime Minister Margaret Thatcher call those American ships, 'flagships of freedom', and immediately I sat down and wrote a poem":

Flagships of Freedom

Sail the open seas
Carrying cargo o'er the world
For folks like you and me

Crude oil from the Persian Gulf
Cars from far Japan
Wood from forests of the world
Crews work hand and hand

Keep the sea lanes open
Let commerce flow quite free
Sail on, sail on
You flagship proud,
For the cause of liberty

Andrea sent this poem to the Prime Minister, and he received an acknowledgment of gratitude for his support and compliment.

Andrea's greatest pleasure was writing poetry on the sea and the admirable ships that sailed the waters and defended her country. "A poem is a story, a condensed novel," he said in an interview. "I write poems and give them to people to open their minds". He wrote about Navy ships to heighten awareness and tell their story and honor their contributions, so their history and legacy may never be forgotten.

Torpedo Boats – Expendable

Expendable. Such is your glory.
History writes the brilliant story.
Sleek, fast boats with speed tremendous,
Destruction packed with force stupendous.

Great carriers you caused to falter
And the course of history alter.
Where your sights for targets sought,
Mighty ships were found and caught

You paved the bottom of the sea
With tokens of your victory
Expendable. Such is your story.
Torpedo boats, now gone to glory

Navy Flying Boat (PBY)

Flying boat, vigilant, sure
Weather and distance you endure
Hovering, hovering night and day
Keeping enemy subs away
Convoys hear your motors drone
Many the missions you have flown
To keep our shipping safe afloat
With all the cargoes that they tote
In victory we hail your name
PBY, you've earned your fame

Fighting Submarine

Men who fight beneath the sea,
Attack their foe then swiftly flee
With fish of tin they blast their mark
Leaving the vanquished to the stalking shark
By secret code the message is in
"Ready!" "Dive!" pumps begin
"Stand by all tubes!" "Ready!" "Fire."
The enemy's ship is blown higher and higher
This is war and no mistake
The enemy fleet must surely break
Convoys of ships with war supplies
Must founder before the periscope's eyes
All must yield to the hidden might
That stalks the sea, day and night.

The Helm That They Herald Is No More

The helm that they herald is no more
The ship lies still on the ocean's floor
A thousand dreams have foundered there
The day was filled with fight and despair
For fight and despair there is much to say
This dauntless ship made the enemy pay
Six sunken subs, two cruisers too
A score of planes wish they never flew
The fight was fierce, the end came fast
We fought and fired till the last
The last will never come again
The ship will live in lasting fame

Christopher Columbus

$\mathcal{A}$ndrea Lippi had such a profound respect and admiration for the great navigator, Christopher Columbus, he felt compelled to write numerous poems, telling of his famous voyage, praising every detail.

Perhaps the most famous explorer of all time, Andrea was fascinated with Columbus' perseverance and visionary genius. He did a great amount of research and travel to understand his life, his ships and his legacy.

In 1956, Andrea started his quest by visiting Genoa, Italy, Columbus' birthplace and childhood home. As he stood outside the doors of the house, he posed for a keepsake photo and embraced the joy of being at that very spot. The home has been made a national monument by the Italian government.

The mission of Christopher Columbus in 1492 was to find a faster sea route to Asia by sailing westward across the Atlantic. His stumbling upon the Caribbean was pure accident. In February of 1957, Andrea visited San Salvador Island in the Bahamas. He met with Commissioner N.E. Bodield, who took Andrea to the very spot where Columbus first came ashore and planted the Spanish Flag. The stretch of beach had a pure, serene atmosphere and held only a simple large-scale cross and an obelisk that served as an impressive monument to this amazing feat.

Andrea was so moved on the beach in San Salvador, he vowed to recreate the landing site on a particular stretch of beach in Cape May. He tried for years but found opposition from Cape May officials.

Andrea's most renowned poem on Columbus is simply titled "The Discovery".

The Discovery

In the year of 1492
Three ships sailed westward in the blue

On and on they sailed afar
With the help of God, a chart and a star

The winds and the storms did their part
To make this voyage a work of art

Columbus, Captain of the three
Changed the course of history

The Queen of Spain, so the story's told
Gave her jewels that they be sold

To buy the ships and pay the crew
A regal deed of a woman true

Was after midnight and the hour of two
A look-out spied this land so new

History changed that very hour
The world then blossomed like a flower

A nation strong across the sea
America…where men are free

In one of his poems on Columbus, Andrea would pay tribute to Queen Isabella. He recognized that Columbus would never have set out on his voyage of exploration and discovery without her, and her king's financial backing and support.

In another poem, Andrea, a mariner himself, pays tribute to the famous sailing ships of Columbus.

AMERICAN FUTURE

Columbus without Isabella
Would never have left the beach
Without the gold and jewels so rare
No new world would be reached

Was the hand of God
Acting with the noble Spanish Queen
That set the sails and moved the wind
That a new land would be seen

The New Land is America
A country strong and true
What happens to its future
Is up to me and you

SANTA MARIA

Was the Eve of Christmas
Not all went well
Santa Maria wrecked
Cracked like a Shell

The helmsman faltered
Sea claimed her prize
All was really
A blessing in disguise

The Flagship eastward
Could not sail
Never against
The winter storm and gale

Nina and Pinta
Not so Big
Could sail into the wind
Their sheets a different rig

Columbus reached Spain
The story then told
Of an Admiral and a Dream
A new world to unfold.

1992 was the 500th Anniversary of the maiden voyage, and Andrea was energized with excitement. In May of that year, he went on a Good-Will visit to Spain sponsored by Air Europa and Spanish Heritage Tours commemorating the anniversary.

Andrea had a special love for Spain for many reasons. One of which was the crucial role Spain and Queen Isabella played in the success of Columbus. Andrea's love for Spain can be felt in this poem:

Vision of a Poet
"Spain"

Oh Spain you seem to talk to me

And tell me a gallant tale

Of stories bold and long ago

Armadas that did sail

Of armies and of navies

Emperors, Dons and Kings

Of a Queen and a lonely Captain

Who shared with them a dream

All this, Dear Spain, I hear from you

With words that go through time

God has made thy beautiful

And made me part of thine.

Christopher Columbus

Andrea's trip to Spain was a successful Cultural/Trade trip where Andrea met with several dignitaries and presented them with an Isabella/Columbus Commemorative Medal and a copy of the poem "Discovery", as well as other Americana memorabilia.

Andrea with the Honorable Miguel Escalona Quesada, Mayor of Torremolinos, Spain.

The Honorable Esperanza Ona Seville, Mayor of Fuengirola, Spain, showing with pride the Isabella/Columbus Medal.

Andrea with Liz Parry, writer for SUR newspaper. Andrea was a supporter of the newspaper for English speaking citizens in the South of Spain.

Andrea with the Mayor of Torremolinos, Spain, Pedro Fernandez Montes. The Honorable Mayor Montes has done outstanding work for the city and for its people in his many years in office.

For the occasion of the 500th Anniversary of the Columbus voyage, the Spanish government built full-size replicas of the Nina, the Pinta and the Santa Maria. These ships left Spain and sailed the ocean blue to "The New World" to recreate the voyage.

When *La Nina* came to the port at Camden, N.J. on its tour, Andrea was there and presented Vincent Sarubbi, Camden County Freeholder, with the Isabella-Columbus medal. Hon. Sarubbi and the commander of the ship, Captain Spangler Morgan, were also presented with Andrea's poem, "The Discovery", in the spirit of Columbus 500.

There is much controversy over Christopher Columbus and his title of "discovering America", but there is no doubting that extraordinary changes resulted from his voyages that altered human history on a global scale.

It was probable that Andrea related to Columbus in many different aspects. Both were Italian, both were dreamers, both were religious, and both were persistent in the sharing of themselves for the good of the world and what they believed in. Andrea wrote many poems on Christopher Columbus and the voyage; the passion can be read and felt in every line. Here are just a few:

The Courage of Columbus

The courage of Columbus
Is what we need today
With the obstacles
That mar our path
There's one thing we can say

Sail on! Sail on!
Oh! Ship of faith
Sail on! All shipmates too
Remember, the courage of Columbus
God also has given you.

Columbus's Prayer

Lord deliver me to the land far away
The very land they call Cathay

Where gold and jewels and spices rare
Are there for the very world to share

That my queen might be pleased with me
When the treasures she does see

God in heaven there on high
We worship thee beneath heavens sky

Columbus Wish
From his ship's bunk where he lay
In a dream he envisioned Cathay

A land so full of beauty rare
His very being did enchant the air

Heaven and paradise are like this all
I hope to enter when angels call

Behold In A Crystal

There in a crystal
So the story is told
Of a great new land
They did behold

Richer and wiser
With expanse so great
The very vision
Sealed their fate

Ships and men
Did travel far
Guided by
A sacred star

Columbus and Isabella
Made a dream come true
A blessed land
For me and you

A. Lippi

Brave Columbus

Brave Columbus did He not sail west
On one of man's most remarkable quests

Followed the sun to a land so new
With but a star and a chosen crew

With a Queen to pray to God on high
That fair winds would blow from a friendly sky

And he would return to the Spanish shore
And man would revere him for evermore

In Andrea's dream to recreate the San Salvador memorial, he built a model of an obelisk in dedication to Christopher Columbus and Queen Isabella.

Andrea was never able to utilize this model for the Columbus memorial he wished for, but little did he know at that time, this model would serve an even greater tribute.

After Andrea's death in 2000, his wife, Catherine, struggled to find an appropriate stone befitting a man of passion and romance. Catherine pondered for a very long time, looking for a sign or something to 'call' her. One morning, with a little help from above, it came to her clear as could be…the Obelisk!

A. Lippi

A few months after this revelation, Catherine found a note written by Andrea, tucked away under a stack of his papers and poems. It was on a yellow scrap of paper and stuck out from the pile as if calling to Catherine.

It read:

Seek the highest land you find
Then go with true peace of mind
Build for me 'neath heaven sky
An obelisk that will reach on high.

This was confirmation for Catherine
that Andrea's wish was done.

Catherine had the obelisk Andrea created for Christopher
Columbus and Queen Isabella constructed in Granite.
On the stone were carved his most treasured words.

On the west side of the obelisk,
there is a rainbow and underneath it reads:

"The Half has not been told".

On the east is carved this poem he wrote:

Perseverance has no boundaries.
Steady progress fires its foundries.
The iron-clad will reap its own reward:
Faith in yourself, trust in the Lord.

Andrea always spoke those words of wisdom in his conversations. He felt that perseverance was the secret to success. He very much associated those words with Christopher Columbus; for if Columbus hadn't persevered in his dream of discovering new lands, our world may not be as we know it.

Andrea used to say,

"Through perseverance, worlds were discovered."

The obelisk sits proudly on Andrea's resting place at the notable Cold Spring Cemetery in New Jersey, awaiting to be moved to his family plot at the prestigious and historic Laurel Hill Cemetery in Philadelphia, Pennsylvania.

Andrea Lippi, a believer of the mystic, rests with a stone that harmonizes with his life, his enthusiasm and his message.

$\mathcal{M}$uch can be said about Andrea and Catherine's loving marriage, for it was a fairy tale romance from beginning to end. From the time they met in 1970, they were inseparable, and enjoyed each other's company immensely. They were soul mates in every sense of the word, and they had a mutual respect for each other and a sincere devotion that kept them strong for 30 years.

Andrea adored 'Ketty' and wrote many poems pledging his love. These next poems are only a glimpse of the many he wrote for his wife, whom he called 'Bear'. Their inspiring and fascinating love story and poetry we shall leave for a possible future book.

That Forgotten Bygone Land

When I am with you there is no despair
But only music in the air
When I am with you the stars all shine
Because they all know that you are mine

When I am with you and hold your hand
The world is all a magic land
Did I walk by and touch your hand
In some forgotten bygone land?

Another time, that we did know
Yet feel that it was long ago
Would I but have a crystal ball
To look and see and know it all

Life's great secrets, young and old
Would suddenly do unfold...
That I walked by and touched your hand
In that forgotten bygone land

Little Dutch Girl that I love
You are sent by heaven above
All the world for you I see
Hoping that you belong to me

Andrea wrote that poem when they first met.

I know the magic mountain
That lies beyond the sea
I know it for your every kiss
Has brought it here to me

You are the magic mountain
From the land beyond the stars
I am King and you my Queen
In this wondrous world of ours

Remembering Andrea ...

*My friend Andrea Lippi....
a ray of sunshine on a cloudy day.....*

*In the twenty years that we maintained our
friendship, he never failed to delight and cheer
me with his spontaneous phone calls, visits,
notes and most of all, his captivating poetry.*

*The sound of his voice always lifted my
spirits and brought a smile to my lips.*

*He always had a vision to the future, a sense
of all that was good and positive in life and a
desire to share his beautiful spirit with the world.*

*Ketty has kept his spirit alive in the hearts and
minds of all of us whose lives he touched,
and we are all better for having known him.*

God Bless you Andrea, until we meet again.

Mona Raskin

I have known Andrea Lippi for at least 45 years and have always considered him to be one of my best friends. Even though we were hundreds of miles apart, we communicated regularly by telephone and mail.

He was one of the most decent, courteous and respectful persons I have ever known, and I know that he has gone to a better place.

I do miss him very much every day of my life.

Herman Jones

In reflecting on my relationship with Andrea, I remember our long conversations, his beloved sea lands and his insight for a bright future.

His poems were most enlightening and he always brought copies to our office and signed each one to the girls and myself.

He is greatly missed.

Mr. Harry N. Hand

Andrea was a wonderful person, and I
have so many fond memories of him.

I still have the wonderful poems he would
give me whenever he came to my office.
We always talked about Italy and
he would say to me, "Angela, I'm going to
take you to beautiful Italy someday".

Angela Pulvino

There are so many fond memories of my good and
faithful friend, Andrea Lippi, that are overwhelming.

Andrea had a unique talent, a psychic ability, to analyze
a situation or person, and within minutes, compose a poem
so appropriate, as to dazzle the imagination.

As U.S. Overseas Airlines Public Relations Director,
Andrea delighted and amused the crewmembers
and the general public with his amazing personality.

He was a true American Patriot and is,
and will be, sorely missed.

Ralph Cox D.D.S.

Lise is a long-time friend of the Lippi's. She is an accomplished writer and artist and wrote these beautiful words for Andrea in Spanish, translated below.

Today is your Birthday,
and the sky has a thousand stars.

But only one star shines brighter than the rest,
and this is your star.

With love you are in our memories for eternity.
This day is yours, and we love you very much .

Lisal Shupbach

Andre was always calling me extolling his patriotism.

In the over twenty years of conversations I came
to realize that he taught me the true meaning
of love for your family and country.

I sorely miss those discussions.

John J. Murray CPA

I became acquainted with Andrea because he
had been a decades-long friend of my father's.
His vocation as "POET" fit him perfectly,
since he was the eternal optimist.

I got the feeling that, through his poetry,
Andrea tried to make sense of an increasingly
unsettled and unsettling world.

He always sought the positive in people
and in situations and was always
UPBEAT and HOPEFUL.

Antonia "Toni" Plick

❦ *Credits* ❦

Ketty's Page

I am so unbelievably happy to share the life of my husband and his poetry. My hope is that young people benefit from his wisdom and catch his spark and spontaneity, which delighted the hearts of so many people.

His memory lives on in these pages.

I would like to thank all the kind people who made this book possible: My friends at the copy center, Deborah P., Diana S., Matthew U. and Amelia E.; my friends at the photo lab, John H., Marie H. and Robin G.; the staff at the library in C.M.C.H.; the two young men, Joshua L.-H. and Lucas H., and so many more, all who diligently and patiently helped me in my efforts to compile this book.

I would also like to thank Tom Phelan, Esq. and his family for their support and friendship over the years.

I would especially like to thank and acknowledge the talent and dedication of the authors, Mik and Maria Kane, who far exceeded all my expectations. It was a joy and a pleasure to work with them on this book.

Story Credits

In writing this book, I read hundreds of articles and newspaper clippings about Andrea that were written throughout his life. I read them over and over and over again. Every word helped me build a truer sense of the man and his accomplishments. The articles Andrea wrote for his newspapers were, by far, my foundation in writing style, and I love him for his intimate and carefree way of composition. But I would like to acknowledge the work of other writers and journalists who so eloquently wrote about Andrea.

I would especially like to thank Barbara St. Claire, for her articles, which I referred to time and time again. A special mention to Toni Plick and Maureen Harris for their personal support and enthusiasm

I would also like to thank Kathy and David Bayard and Tom Phelan for their help in editing, and a special thank you to Paul and Crystal Combitsis.

Also, to my husband, Mik, thank you for being so amazingly creative. I adore you.

In appreciation for the support of Andrea throughout the years:

The Armed Forces

Philadelphia Exclusive, PA
Philadelphia Inquirer, PA
Atlantic City Press, NJ
Cape May Star and Wave, NJ
Gazette Leader of Cape May, NJ
Herald Lantern Dispatch, Rio Grande, NJ
Ocean City Record, NJ
Shoppe Publications, Villas, NJ
WSNJ Radio, Bridgeton, NJ
WCNC TV Channel 40, Wildwood, NJ

Credits

Picture Credits

Ace Alagara
Mike Blizzard
Al Campbell
Barbara St. Claire
Foto Buro Lex Sal Verda
Foto Leoni
Sue Frederiksen
David Gath
Gazette Leader
Herald Lantern Dispatch
Thomas Kinnemand
Lesley
Library of Congress
Andrea Lippi
Joseph McGuinn
K. Meesters
Walter O'Brien
National Gallery of Art
Ed Palaez

Port Authority of Philadelphia
Press Agency Widdershoven
Kris Proctor
Eugene Armen Rai
Jim Raftery - Turfotos
Regina Studios
San Francisco Maritime Museum
Scandinavian Air System
Ed Scheetz
M. Schubert
Carl Seibert
South Jersey Living Magazine
South Jersey News Service
United Press Photos - Rome
United States Army
United States Coast Guard
United States Navy
Doris Ward
World News International

Two A's Had I On My Report

Two A's had I on my report
But these were A's of another sort

Beginning and ending with my name
These A's were my only claim of fame

To roam the world I did quite well
Though surely I could never spell

But poems adopted me for their very own
As a vagabond king I share a throne

"POET"